I0438716

Spring and Summer Spatial Distribution of Endangered Juvenile Lost River and Shortnose Suckers in Relation to Environmental Variables in Upper Klamath Lake, Oregon: 2007 Annual Report

By Summer M. Burdick and Scott P. VanderKooi, U.S. Geological Survey, and Greer O. Anderson, National Oceanic and Atmospheric Administration

Prepared in cooperation with the Bureau of Reclamation

Open-File Report 2009-1043

U.S. Department of the Interior
U.S. Geological Survey

U.S. Department of the Interior
KEN SALAZAR, Secretary

U.S. Geological Survey
Suzette M. Kimball, Acting Director

U.S. Geological Survey, Reston, Virginia: 2009

For more information on the USGS—the Federal source for science about the Earth, its natural and living resources, natural hazards, and the environment, visit http://www.usgs.gov or call 1-888-ASK-USGS.

For an overview of USGS information products, including maps, imagery, and publications, visit *http://www.usgs.gov/pubprod*

To order this and other USGS information products, visit *http://store.usgs.gov*

Contents

Conversion Factors and Abbreviations and Acronyms

SI to Inch/Pound

Multiply	By	To obtain
Length		
centimeter (cm)	0.3937	inch (in.)
millimeter (mm)	0.03937	inch (in.)
meter (m)	3.281	foot (ft)
kilometer (km)	0.6214	mile (mi)
Area		
square meter (m^2)	10.76	square foot (ft^2)
Volume		
liter (L)	0.2642	gallon (gal)
Mass		
gram (g)	0.03527	ounce, avoirdupois (oz)
kilogram (kg)	2.205	pound avoirdupois (lb)

Temperature in degrees Celsius (°C) may be converted to degrees Fahrenheit (°F) as follows:
$$°F=(1.8×°C)+32.$$

Temperature in degrees Fahrenheit (°F) may be converted to degrees Celsius (°C) as follows:
$$°C=(°F-32)/1.8.$$

Concentrations of chemical constituents in water are given either in milligrams per liter (mg/L) or micrograms per liter (µg/L).

Abbreviations and Acronyms

Abbreviations	Meaning
SL	standard length
SE	standard error
PIT	passive integrated transponder
CPUE	catch per unit effort
DO	dissolved oxygen
USGS	U.S. Geological Survey
AIC	Akaike's Information Criteria
AICc	Akaike's Information Criteria adjusted for small sample size
QAICc	quasi- Akaike's Information Criteria

Spring and Summer Spatial Distribution of Endangered Juvenile Lost River and Shortnose Suckers in Relation to Environmental Variables in Upper Klamath Lake, Oregon: 2007 Annual Report

By Summer M. Burdick[1], Scott P. VanderKooi[2], and Greer O. Anderson[3]

Executive Summary

Lost River sucker *Deltistes luxatus* and shortnose sucker *Chasmistes brevirostris* were listed as endangered in 1988 for a variety of reasons including apparent recruitment failure. Upper Klamath Lake, Oregon, and its tributaries are considered the most critical remaining habitat for these two species. Age-0 suckers are often abundant in Upper Klamath Lake throughout the summer months, but catches decline dramatically between late August and early September each year, and age-1 and older subadult suckers are rare. These rapid declines in catch rates and a lack of substantial recruitment into adult sucker populations in recent years suggests sucker populations experience high mortality between their first summer and first spawn. A lack of optimal rearing habitat may exacerbate juvenile sucker mortality or restrict juvenile growth or development.

In 2007, we continued research on juvenile sucker habitat use begun by the U.S. Geological Survey (USGS) in 2001. Age-0 catch rates in 2006 were more than an order of magnitude greater than in previous years, which prompted us to refocus our research from age-0 sucker to age-1 sucker distributions and habitat use. We took a two-phased approach to our research in 2007 that included preliminary spring sampling and intense summer sampling components. Spring sampling was a pilot study designed to gather baseline data on the distribution of age-1 suckers as they emerge from winter in shoreline environments throughout Upper Klamath Lake (Chapter 1). Whereas, summer sampling was designed to quantitatively estimate the influence of environmental variables on age-0 and age-1 sucker distribution throughout Upper Klamath Lake, while accounting for imperfect detection (Chapter 2). In addition to these two components, we began a project to evaluate passive integrated transponder (PIT) tag loss and the effects of PIT tags on mortality of age-1 Lost River suckers (Chapter 3).

[1] *sburdick@usgs.gov*, U.S. Geological Survey, Klamath Falls, OR
[2] *svanderkooi@usgs.gov*, U.S. Geological Survey, Klamath Falls, OR
[3] *greer.anderson@noaa.gov*, National Oceanic and Atmospheric Administration, Yreka, CA

The spring pilot study built the foundation for future research on post-wintering juvenile sucker distribution and habitat use studies. Only 34 percent of nets set during spring sampling (April 2 to May 29) caught juvenile suckers and catch rates were low (0.038 to 0.405 suckers/hour) and widely distributed throughout shoreline areas. Of 13 suckers sacrificed for identification, only one was determined to be a Lost River sucker. All others were either shortnose suckers or Klamath large-scale *Catostomus snyderi* suckers, but were not identified to species. Suckers caught during the spring averaged 93 ± 2 millimeter (mm) standard length (SL; mean ± SE) and were all estimated to be a year old. Spring catches did not vary in respect to nearness to tributary streams or rivers, substrate type, area of the lake, or distance from shore. However, a higher percentage of nets caught at least one sucker when they were set within 50 meters (m) of a wetland edge (60 percent) compared to nets set 200 m from a wetland (30 percent) or in other shoreline areas (29 percent). Our results also suggest that in the spring age-1 suckers use habitats less than 2 m deep at a greater frequency than deeper environments, a trend that was reversed in the summer.

Temporal trends in summer catch rates of age-0 suckers generally were similar to those in previous years, with a peak during the week of August 5. In contrast, age-1 sucker catches were relatively high until the week of July 16, but rapidly declined each week for the rest of the sampling season. Age-0 suckers were caught at higher rates than age-1 suckers though the summer, but both age groups were captured at a similar percentage of sites (age-0, 26.5 percent and age-1, 27.4 percent). Age-0 catches were composed of slightly more Lost River suckers (53.2 percent) than shortnose suckers (42.1 percent). In contrast, most age-1 suckers were shortnose suckers (72.7 percent).

Our summer sampling indicates that age-0 suckers within Upper Klamath Lake primarily are habitat generalists, whereas age-1 sucker habitat use varied slightly with water depth. Age-0 suckers were most likely to use shallow (1 to 3 m) water widely available in Upper Klamath Lake throughout the summer; age-1 suckers were most likely to use deeper (4 to 5 m) water environments in the summer, which are diminished at lower lake-surface elevations. This depth selection for age-1 suckers is similar to that of adult suckers, which are known to concentrate at water depths 3 m or greater.

Despite extensive research on Lost River and shortnose suckers, relatively little information exists on juvenile survival, movement, growth rates, and age to maturity. We therefore evaluated the viability of using Passive Integrated Transponder (PIT) tag technology for researching these issues. We determined that 12.5 mm PIT tags are a viable option for studying movement and mortality rates of Lost River suckers of at least 75 mm SL. However, any estimates of natural mortality that are generated from PIT tagging studies will need to be adjusted for tagging mortality, which was 9.8 percent in our laboratory experiment and 17.5 percent in overnight field trials, and for tag loss, which was 2.1 percent in the laboratory and 5.0 percent in field trials. Post-tagging necropsies indicated that mortality may be reduced if effort is made to improve tagger skill through practice. Therefore, tagging mortality should be reassessed within any natural mortality studies on juvenile suckers that use this technology. New, smaller (8.0 mm) tags also should be assessed to determine their effect on mortality rates.

Chapter 1.—Spring Shoreline Distribution of Age-1 Suckers in Upper Klamath Lake, Oregon

By Summer M. Burdick, U.S. Geological Survey, Greer O. Anderson, National Oceanic and Atmospheric Administration, and Scott P. VanderKooi, U.S. Geological Survey

Introduction

Recruitment failure is cited as one of the major causes for the decline in endangered Lost River sucker *Deltistes luxatus* and shortnose sucker *Chasmistes brevirostris* populations in Upper Klamath Lake, Oregon (National Research Council, 2004). Dramatic declines in age-0 catch rates between late August and early September each year combined with extremely low catches of age-1 or older suckers in Upper Klamath Lake, Oregon (Hendrixson and others, 2007), suggest these species experience unusually high mortality during their first autumn and winter. High autumn and winter mortality may be exacerbated by a lack of optimal winter habitat, which may be needed for suckers to recover from low fall energy reserves (Foott and Stone, 2005). One way to examine the value of lake environments for reducing over-wintering mortality is to examine the spatial distribution of post-winter catch rates. In-lake environments producing higher catch rates of surviving juvenile suckers are assumed to provide better winter habitat.

A limited amount of available data suggests post-wintering (spring) and early summer distributions of juvenile suckers are concentrated in tributary mouths and near springs. Between April 21 and May 11, 1992, Markle and Simon (1993) caught a relatively high number of age-1 and older subadult suckers (76) in overnight trap nets set in tributaries at the northern end of Upper Klamath Lake. However, they caught few in trap nets set offshore during the same time period (4) or in offshore otter trawls conducted each spring since 1996 (fewer than 20 between 1996 and 2006; Simon and others, 2000a; Simon and others, 2000b; Simon and Markle, 2001, 2002, 2006; Terwilliger and others, 2008). U.S. Geological Survey (USGS) employees also caught age-1 suckers near the mouth of the Williamson River and at the springs along the eastern shore in early July between 2004 and 2006 (Hendrixson and others, 2007; Burdick and others, 2008a). Age-1 and older suckers may be selecting springs and tributaries because of their unique water chemistry, warmer winter temperatures, or winter productivity, but none of these hypotheses has been tested.

In the spring of 2007, we conducted low intensity sampling to document post-wintering shoreline distributions of age-1 and older suckers in Upper Klamath Lake. Higher than average catch rates of young-of-the-year suckers in 2006 (Burdick and others, 2008a) suggested a greater possibility of catching more age-1 suckers than in previous years. This general survey was intended to expand basic knowledge about spring juvenile sucker distributions. Information gained from this portion of the study provides a better understanding of post-wintering juvenile sucker distributions, which can be used to make inferences about where these species over-winter, and will help guide more intensive studies in the future.

Knowledge about distribution of age-0 and adult Lost River and shortnose sucker habitat helped guide our spring sampling effort for age-1 suckers in 2007. Age-0 suckers use nearshore and offshore lake environments (Hendrixson and others, 2007). Catch rates for age-0 suckers in trap nets are approximately equally distributed between vegetated marshes and unvegetated lake environments (Hendrixson and others, 2007). During their first summer, suckers use shallow water (Burdick and others, 2008b) with small substrates including mud and sand (Buettner and Scoppettone, 1990; Hendrixson and others, 2007), as well as lake environments with larger substrates including cobble and gravel (Terwilliger and others, 2004; Hendrixson and others, 2007). Adult suckers, however, are most frequently found in deeper (3 to 4 m) unvegetated areas (Banish and others, 2009). The age at which suckers transition from using shallow and sometimes vegetated lake environments to deeper unvegetated areas has yet to be determined. In this chapter, we describe the spatial and temporal distribution of age-1 sucker catches in Upper Klamath Lake during the spring of 2007.

Methods

Collection of Samples

Eighteen sites around the perimeter of Upper Klamath Lake were chosen for spring sampling (April 2 to May 29) using a combination of previous knowledge about spring age-1 sucker distribution and professional judgment (fig. 1). Three sites were sampled each week with two trap nets set overnight (mean soak time of 24.6 ± SE 1.6 hours) at each site. Trap nets were constructed with 6.4 mm delta mesh with a lead (1.2 m deep × 16 m long) and rectangular frame (1.2 × 1.8 m) mounted to four circular hoops (1 m diameter, 1 m apart) and containing three internal fykes. Nets were set at 50 and 200 m from shore, in line with each other, and perpendicular to the shoreline with leads facing inland. A total of 54 trap net sets were completed in three separate areas of the lake for a total sampling effort of 1,326.2 hours soak time. The three areas of the lake were: (1) north and west of Eagle Point and the mouth of the Williamson River (North), (2) south and east of Eagle Point and the mouth of the Williamson River and north of Squaw Point and Hagelstein Park (Central), (3) south of Hagelstein Park and Squaw Point including Howard Bay (South; fig. 1). Trap net sets were distributed approximately equally among the three areas (North = 16, Central = 18, South = 20).

Captured fish were identified to species and counted. Standard length (SL) was measured for all suckers. When catches, weighed in cod end of net with a spring scale, exceeded 2 to 3 kg, a subsample was taken for all species except juvenile suckers. Prior to subsampling, the presence and absence of each non-sucker species was recorded in one of two size bins (small, <100 mm SL; large, ≥ 100 mm SL). Subsamples were taken by placing the entire sample in a large water-filled tub, thoroughly mixing the contents of the tub, and removing about 30 percent of the original sample weight using a dip net. All fish in the subsample were identified to species and counted. Subsample species composition was assumed representative of total catch. The total number of each species in the catch was estimated by extrapolation using the ratio of subsample weight to total weight.

Approximately 1 in 10 suckers were sacrificed and later frozen for identification to species. Juvenile suckers were identified as either Lost River suckers, or a grouping of shortnose and Klamath largescale *Catostomus snyderi* suckers, using vertebral counts as described by (Markle and others, 2005). Sacrificed suckers also were used in a related but separate pilot study on triglyceride content, which required them to remain frozen. Therefore, gill raker counts needed to further separate shortnose from Klamath largescale suckers were not conducted. Given that juvenile Klamath largescale suckers are infrequent in catches throughout the lake (Hendrixson and others, 2007), we assumed that most fish in this grouping were shortnose rather than Klamath largescale suckers. We further assumed that the identified portion of sucker species was representative of the total catch.

4

GIS Analysis and Mapping Techniques

We used ArcMap 9.2 to associate our sample sites with site characteristics such as wetlands, tributaries, and substrates. A substrate class was assigned to each site by using Hawth's Analysis Tools (Beyer, 2006) to link our sample locations to sonar substrate data from Eliers and Eliers (2007). We simplified Eliers and Eliers (2007) substrate classes into two groups, small (mud, clay, or sand) and large (gravel, cobble, rock and boulder) for our analysis. We additionally classified sites as being either adjacent (≤ 200 m) or distant (> 200 m) from tributaries and wetland edges (USGS 7.5-minute topographic maps). ArcGIS software also was used to examine temporal and spatial patterns in sucker distribution.

Summary and Analysis of Data

We summarized and analyzed data collected in spring 2007 on the basis of a variety of questions related to temporal and spatial abundance and distribution, and species composition. We calculated catch per unit effort (CPUE; fish/hour) for juvenile suckers and summarized it based on location, date, and substrate type. Specifically, we looked at the distribution of suckers in relation to site characteristics such as location within the lake (North, Central, or South), distance from shore (50 or 200 m), proximity to wetlands (> 200, 200, or 50 m), proximity to tributary streams or rivers (adjacent or distant), substrate size (small or large), and water depth (<2, 2–3, 3–4, and >4 m). For all comparisons, we assumed constant capture efficiency among all spring net sets. Test statistics were inappropriate for these data, given small sample sizes and the frequency of nets that caught no suckers. Therefore, we took a qualitative and exploratory approach in summarizing these data.

Results

We caught a total of 53 juvenile suckers during 9 weeks of trap netting in Upper Klamath Lake in spring 2007. Of the 54 trap net sets during this time period, 35 percent contained juvenile suckers but only 19 percent caught more than one sucker. In the nets that did catch suckers, CPUE ranged from 0.038 to 0.405. The highest mean daily catch rate occurred on May 29 (0.16 ± 0.07) and the lowest mean catch rate occurred on May 7, when no suckers were caught over a combined total of 146.5 hours of soak time (fig. 2). The net with the single highest catch rate (0.405 fish/hour) was set 50 m off Squaw Point Marsh in Howard Bay on May 29 and had a catch rate 1.67 times greater than the next most productive net set.

A total of 13 suckers were kept for identification to species. Of these, six were mortalities that occurred during a tagging experiment (see Chapter 3), one was a mortality attributed to a lamprey, one was found dead at the Running Y boat ramp on the southwest shore, and five were sacrificed to characterize the species composition in our catches. Only one of these suckers was positively identified as a Lost River Sucker. Nine others were identified as either shortnose or Klamath largescale suckers, and the final three were unidentifiable using our methods. The Lost River sucker was captured on May 29 in Howard Bay 50 m off Squaw Point Marsh. The nine fish, identified as either shortnose or Klamath largescale suckers, were captured near Cove Point (3), Howard Bay (3), Moore Park (1), Thompson Creek (1), or the Running Y boat ramp (1).

Suckers caught during spring sampling ranged between 53 and 147 mm SL with a mean of 93 mm SL (± 2 SE; fig. 3). The longest sucker sacrificed for identification (104 mm SL) was the only fish positively identified as a Lost River sucker. Fish identified as either shortnose or Klamath largescale suckers ranged from 70 to 91 mm SL and averaged 81 ± 2 mm SL. Based on length frequency histograms from all suckers caught in our spring sampling, it is possible that we were able to capture both age-1 and age-2 juvenile suckers, with the two fish larger than 120 mm SL possibly being age-2 fish. Without further evidence as to their ages, however, we assume that these fish were 1-year old and were either born early in the previous year or had higher than average growth rates during their first year. Given that juvenile suckers can reach up to 100 mm SL by the end of their first summer (Markle and Cooperman, 2002), we believe our assumption about the age of these longer fish is reasonable.

There was little variation in the spatial distribution of catch rates for juvenile suckers throughout the lake shore environments sampled in the spring. However, a few minor but notable trends did exist. The percentage of nets to catch at least one sucker was greatest in the south (50 percent), followed by the north (33 percent) and the central (22 percent) portions of the lake. Of the nets that did catch suckers, the highest mean (± SE) CPUE by area occurred in the south (0.12 ± 0.04, n = 10), followed by the central (0.10 ± 0.05; n = 4), and north (0.09 ± 0.02; n = 5) portions of the lake (fig. 4). The percentages of nets to catch at least one sucker were similar between those set 50 m from shore (33 percent) and those set 200 m from shore (37 percent). Additionally, the mean (± SE) CPUE for nets that caught at least one sucker was only slightly greater in nets set at 50 m from shore (0.14 ± 0.04; n=9) than nets set 200 m from shore (0.08 ± 0.02; n=10; fig. 5).

Catches of juvenile suckers differed slightly when nets were set near wetlands as compared to away from them. The percentage of nets that caught at least one sucker was similar between nets set more than 200 m from a wetland (29 percent; n = 34) and those set 200 m from a wetland (30 percent; n = 10). In comparison, the percentage of nets set within 50 m of a wetland that caught at least one sucker (60 percent; n = 10) was at least twice as great. However, the mean CPUE (± SE) in nets that caught at least one sucker was similar at sites 50 m from wetlands (0.12 ± 0.06; n = 6), sites 200 m from wetlands (0.12 ±0.04; n = 3), and sites more than 200 m from wetlands (0.10 ± 0.02; n = 10; fig. 6).

Our catches did not vary greatly across environmental variables such as nearness to tributary streams or rivers, or substrate type. The portion of nets to catch at least one sucker were only slightly greater in nets set adjacent to tributary mouths (40 percent; n = 10) than at sites set away from tributaries (34 percent; n = 44). When only nets that caught at least one sucker were examined, there also was virtually no difference in the mean (± SE) CPUE between those set near tributary mouths (0.10 ± 0.03; n = 4) and those set away from tributary mouths (0.11 ± 0.03; n = 15; fig. 7). A slightly higher percentage of nets set over small substrate (37 percent; n = 40) caught at least one sucker than nets set over large substrate (29 percent; n = 14). One notable difference was in nets that did catch suckers. In these nets, mean (± SE) CPUE was more than twice as high in nets set over small substrate (0.12 ± 0.03) than in nets set over large substrate (0.06 ± 0.02; fig. 8).

Water depth, however, may be a stronger determinant of sucker habitat. Despite our small sample size, we saw a declining trend with water depth in the percentage of trap net sets that caught at least one sucker. Nets set in less than 2 m of water had the highest percentage of positive catches (75 percent; n = 4) followed by those set in 2 to 3 m (43 percent; n = 33) and 3 to 4 m (13 percent; n = 15) of water. Neither of two nets set in water deeper than 4 m caught suckers. This trend was reversed when mean (± SE) catch rates in nets that caught suckers were examined across depth categories. Mean (± SE) CPUE was highest when nets were set at 3 to 4 m deep (0.12 ± 0.08), only slightly lower when set in water 2 to 3 m deep (0.11 ± 0.04) or less than 2 m deep (0.10 ± 0.03; fig. 9).

Our spring catches were fairly diverse but were dominated by three widely distributed species. The order of highest to lowest total CPUE among species was blue chub *Gila coerulea*, followed by tui chub *G. bicolor*, fathead minnow *Pimephales promelas*, Klamath Lake sculpin *Cottus princeps*, yellow perch *Perca flavescens*, Upper Klamath marbled sculpin *Cottus klamathensis klamathensis*, sucker spp., lamprey *Lampetra* spp., unidentified sculpin species *Cottus* spp., pumpkinseed *Lepomis gibbosus*, slender sculpin *Cottus tenuis*, and brown bullhead *Ameiurus nebulosus*. Blue chub had the widest spring distribution and were captured in 91 percent of nets, followed by fathead minnows in 87 percent of nets, Klamath sculpin in 80 percent of nets, and tui chub in 78 percent of nets. The percentages of nets that captured yellow perch (33 percent), marbled sculpin (33 percent), and lamprey (17 percent) were much smaller. Pumpkinseed were captured in only two nets, and slender sculpin and brown bullhead were captured in only one net each.

Overall species composition was similar through time, across areas of the lake, and near or distant from shore, wetlands or tributaries. Total catch rates were highest on April 23 and May 14 and lowest on May 21 and May 29 (fig. 10). Regardless of catch size, the composition of species was similar among weeks (fig. 10). Total catch rates for all species combined were highest in the southern portion and lowest in the northern portion of the lake, but species composition was similar in all three areas (fig. 11). Nets set 50 m from shore caught more fish than nets set 200 m from shore, regardless of distance from wetlands (fig. 12). Nets set away from tributary mouths (> 200 m) caught slightly more fish than nets set near tributaries, but species composition was similar at both types of sites (fig. 13).

There were some differences in total catch rates and species composition across depth categories (< 2, 2–3, 3–4, and > 4 m). Total catches were lowest in nets set in 3 to 4 m of water, and highest in nets set in less than 2 m or more than 4 m of water (fig. 14). Catches in nets set in less than 2 m of water were dominated by blue and tui chubs, whereas catches in nets set in more than 4 m of water were dominated by fathead minnows. Tui chub catch rates were 2.7 times higher in less than 2 m of water than in any other depth category. Fathead minnows in comparison were caught at rates 5.3 times higher in more than 4 m of water. Of the six most common species, yellow perch was the only one not captured in less than 2 m of water. Marbled sculpin catch rates steadily declined with depth, and no marbled sculpin were captured in more than 4 m of water. In contrast, yellow perch catch rates were 9.9 times higher in nets set in more than 4 m of water compared to all nets set in all other depth categories combined.

When we compared nets that caught suckers to nets that did not catch suckers, species composition was similar with one notable exception. Yellow perch were captured in 45 percent of nets that did not catch suckers but in only 10 percent of nets that also caught suckers. Compared to suckers, yellow perch were small and only 1 out of 62 yellow perch captured was more than 100 mm SL.

Spring Distribution of Age-1 Suckers

Despite our increased effort over previous studies (54 net sets for a total of 1,326.2 soak hours) to examine post-wintering juvenile sucker distributions in Upper Klamath Lake, our catches of juvenile suckers remained low. Other studies also reported low catch rates for juvenile suckers in April and May. Markle and Simon (1993) set 27 overnight trap nets (904 soak hours) in the spring of 1992 during April and May, and captured a total of 76 juvenile suckers in tributaries of Upper Klamath Lake, but only 4 in the lake itself. Markle and Simon (1993) attributed small relative catches of suckers when compared to total catch size to the sedentary nature of suckers compared to blue and tui chub. Differences in catchablity among species are certainly a major factor in estimating abundance from catch rates, but consistently low catches of young suckers in passive and active gears suggest the abundance of these fish may truly be low in Upper Klamath Lake during the spring. From 1996 to 2007, researchers at Oregon State University pulled otter trawls in offshore areas of Upper Klamath Lake between April and May (Simon and Markle, 2008). In this long-term monitoring program, seasonal catch rates never exceeded 0.15 suckers per 20-m tow, which indicates that spring abundance of age-1 suckers within Upper Klamath Lake is commonly low.

A comparison between the sucker species composition in our spring 2007 catches and those in the previous summer suggests shortnose suckers may have experienced better over-winter survival than Lost River suckers. The sucker species composition in our spring 2007 sampling was 69.7 percent shortnose or Klamath largescale, 23.1 percent unidentifiable, and only 7.7 percent Lost River. However, in the previous summer age-0 sucker species composition in our nets was 50.1 percent shortnose or

Klamath largescale, 43.4 percent Lost River, and 6.2 percent unidentifiable suckers (Burdick and others, 2008a). Simon and Markle (2008) also reported a similar split between age-0 Lost River (56 percent) and shortnose (44 percent) suckers caught in cast nets in 2006. Assuming our grouping of shortnose and Klamath largescale suckers was made up predominantly of shortnose suckers, this dramatic proportional change suggests differential survival between the two dominant sucker species. It should be noted, however, that this conclusion is based on only 13 sacrificed suckers in the spring of 2007. Given such a weak inference, speculation as to what may have caused differential mortality would be unwise. Future research may further illuminate species specific differences in survival and abundance.

One of the more interesting contrasts in our spring data was that between sucker catch rates near or distant from wetland edges. High catch rates in nets set at the mouth of Thomason Creek (TCK; fig. 1) and in Howard Bay (HWB; fig. 1) strongly influenced this pattern, which may have been the spurious result of analyzing sparse data. However, wetlands may provide protection from redband trout *Oncorhynchus mykiss newberrii*, which are the most likely fish predator of age-1 suckers, due to their large size and piscivorous diet. Redband trout are abundant in Upper Klamath Lake from late autumn to spring. In June, however, most of these fish move into rivers, which may relieve predation pressure on age-1 suckers later in the summer (W. Tenniswood, Oregon Department of Fish and Wildlife, oral commun., 2008). Alternatively, wetland edges may be attractive to age-1 suckers during colder months because they are associated with springs, which may be warmer than the lake water.

Our spring catch rates for juvenile suckers were unexpectedly similar between nets set near and distant from tributary mouths. We expected our catch rates to be higher near tributary mouths based on a 1992 survey by Markle and Simon (1993), who reported catch rates of juvenile suckers 21 times higher in tributaries than in Upper Klamath Lake itself. The difference between our results and those reported by Markle and Simon (1993) may be due to where nets were set in relation to tributaries. Within tributaries, Markle and Simon (1993) set nets at least 100 m upstream of the mouth, with the lead facing downstream and the cod end upstream, targeting upstream spring migrants. By comparison, we detected little to no difference in catches in our nets set in lake environments within 200 m of tributary mouths, and those set distant (> 200 m) from tributaries. Although Markle and Simon's (1993) results suggest age-1 and older juvenile suckers are most likely to be found in tributaries to Upper Klamath Lake during April and May, our results suggest this same age class does not necessarily use lake environments in close proximity to these streams and rivers at a higher rate than other areas within the lake.

The most promising environmental variable for describing spring age-1 sucker habitat may be water depth. In relation to increasing depth, our results show a declining trend in the percentage of nets that caught at least one sucker, but an increasing trend in catch rates when nets that caught no suckers were excluded from the analysis. This combination of trends may suggest that suckers use shallow water with a greater frequency, but are more concentrated in deeper water in April and May. This spring habitat use pattern provides an interesting contrast to that for deeper water summer habitat used by the same age class of juvenile suckers (Chapter 2). Given the exploratory nature of our spring sampling, the relation between sucker habitat and water depth can only be considered preliminary. However, these data provide support for further study of depth effects on spring habitat use by age-1 suckers.

Species composition in our spring sampling was similar to that observed in summer sampling in 2004, 2005, and 2006, except that yellow perch were in lower relative abundance in our spring samples. Given that catches of small (<100 mm SL) yellow perch peak annually around the second or third week of August (Hendrixson and others, 2007; Burdick and others, 2008a), it is not surprising that they were in lower relative abundance in our spring catches. Yellow perch exhibited a relation to depth opposite to that of juvenile suckers and were caught less frequently when suckers were present. Due to the small size of yellow perch captured in our nets, this observation probably is due to differences in habitat preferences rather than competitive exclusion or some other inter-species interaction.

This pilot study built the foundation for future research on post-wintering distributions of juvenile suckers. Trends observed in the spring of 2007 were based on relatively few net sets and suckers caught, and may not be consistent with trends detected in future years of sampling. Future research should focus on validating differential use of across environmental gradients by both endangered lake sucker species, examining differences in over-winter survival and post-wintering distributions between Lost River and shortnose suckers, and tracking the success of the 2006 cohort to adulthood.

References Cited

Banish, N.P., Adams, B.J., Shively, R.S., Mazur, M.M., Beauchamp, D.A., and Wood, T.M., 2009, Distribution and habitat associations of radio-tagged adult Lost River sucker and shortnose sucker in Upper Klamath Lake, Oregon: Transactions of the American Fisheries Society v. 138, no. 1, p. 153-168.

Beyer, H.L., 2006, Hawth's Analysis Tools for ArcGIS: Accessed February 25, 2009, at http://www.spatialecology.com/htools.

Buettner, M., and Scoppettone, G.G., 1990, Life history and status of Catostomids in Upper Klamath Lake, Oregon: Seattle, Wash., U.S. Fish and Wildlife Service, National Fisheries Research Center, contract completion report, 108 p.

Burdick, S.M., Wilkens, A.X., and VanderKooi, S.P., 2008a, Nearshore and offshore habitat use by endangered juvenile Lost River and shortnose suckers in Upper Klamath Lake, Oregon: U.S. Geological Survey Open-File Report 2007-1356, 30 p.

Burdick, S.M., Hendrixson, H.A., and VanderKooi, S.P., 2008b, Age-0 Lost River and shortnose sucker nearshore habitat use in Upper Klamath Lake, Oregon: A patch-occupancy approach: Transactions of the American Fisheries Society, v. 137, p. 417-430.

Eliers, J.M., and Eliers, B.J., 2007, Fish habitat analysis of Upper Klamath Lake and Agency Lake, Oregon – completion report to Bureau of Reclamation, Klamath Falls, Oregon: Bend, Oreg., J.C. Headwaters, Inc., 37 p.

Foott, J.S., and Stone, R., 2005, FY2004 Report – Bio-energetic and histological evaluation of juvenile (0+) sucker fry from Upper Klamath Lake collected in August and September 2004: Anderson, Calif., U.S. Fish and Wildlife Service California-Nevada Fish Health Center.

Hendrixson, H.A., Burdick, S.M., Wilkens, A.X., and VanderKooi, S.P., 2007, Nearshore and offshore habitat use by endangered, juvenile Lost River and shortnose suckers in Upper Klamath Lake, Oregon – Annual Report 2005: U.S. Geological Survey, Western Fisheries Research Center, Klamath Falls Field Station.

Markle, D.F., and Cooperman, M.S., 2002, Relationships between Lost River and shortnose sucker biology and management of Upper Klamath Lake, in Braunworth, W.S., Welch, T., and Hathaway, R., eds., Water allocation in the Klamath reclamation project, 2001: an assessment of natural resource, economic, social, and institutional issues in the Upper Klamath Basin: Corvallis, Oreg., Oregon State University Extension Service, p. 93-117.

Markle, D.F., and Simon, D.C., 1993, Preliminary studies of systematics and juvenile ecology of Upper Klamath Lake suckers – Final report: Corvallis, Oreg., Oregon State University, Department of Fisheries and Wildlife, 129 p.

Markle, D.F., Cavalluzzi, M.R., and Simon, D.C., 2005, Morphology and taxonomy of Klamath Basin suckers (Catostomidae): Western North American Naturalist, v. 65, no. 4, p. 473-489.

National Research Council, 2004, Endangered and threatened fishes in the Klamath River Basin: Washington, D.C., The National Academies Press, 397 p.

Simon, D.C., and Markle, D.F., 2001, Ecology of Upper Klamath Lake shortnose and Lost River suckers – Annual survey of abundance and distribution of age-0 shortnose and Lost River suckers in Upper Klamath Lake, 2000 annual report: Corvallis, Oreg., Oregon Cooperative Research Unit, Department of Fisheries and Wildlife, Oregon State University.

Simon, D.C., and Markle, D.F., 2002, Ecology of Upper Klamath Lake shortnose and Lost River suckers – Annual survey of abundance and distribution of age-0 shortnose and Lost River suckers in Upper Klamath Lake, 2001 Annual Report: Corvallis, Oreg., Oregon Cooperative Research Unit, Department of Fisheries and Wildlife, Oregon State University.

Simon, D.C., and Markle, D.F., 2006, Ecology of Upper Klamath Lake shortnose and Lost River suckers – Annual survey of abundance and distribution of age-0 shortnose and Lost River suckers in Upper Klamath Lake, 2005 annual report: Corvallis, Oreg., Oregon Cooperative Research Unit, Department of Fisheries and Wildlife, Oregon State University.

Simon, D.C., and Markle, D.F., 2008, Ecology of Upper Klamath Lake shortnose and Lost River suckers – Annual survey of abundance and distribution of age-0 shortnose and Lost River suckers in Upper Klamath Lake, 2007 annual report: Corvallis, Oreg., Oregon Cooperative Research Unit, Department of Fisheries and Wildlife, Oregon State University.

Simon, D.C., Terwilliger, M.R., Murtaugh, P., and Markle, D.F., 2000a, Larval and juvenile ecology of Upper Klamath Lake suckers, 1995–1998: Corvallis, Oreg., Department of Fisheries and Wildlife, Oregon State University.

Simon, D.C., Terwilliger, M.R., and Markle, D.F., 2000b, Ecology of Upper Klamath Lake shortnose and Lost River suckers – Annual survey of abundance and distribution of age-0 shortnose and Lost River suckers in Upper Klamath Lake, 1999 annual report: Corvallis, Oreg., Oregon Cooperative Research Unit, Department of Fisheries and Wildlife, Oregon State University.

Terwilliger, M.R., Simon, D.C., and Markle, D.F., 2004, Larval and juvenile ecology of Upper Klamath Lake suckers, 1995-2003: Corvallis, Oreg., Oregon Cooperative Research Unit, Department of Fisheries and Wildlife, Oregon State University.

Terwilliger, M.R., Simon, D.C., and Markle, D.F., 2008, Ecology of Upper Klamath Lake Shortnose and Lost River Suckers, 2006 annual report: Corvallis, Oreg., Oregon Cooperative Research Unit, Department of Fisheries and Wildlife, Oregon State University.

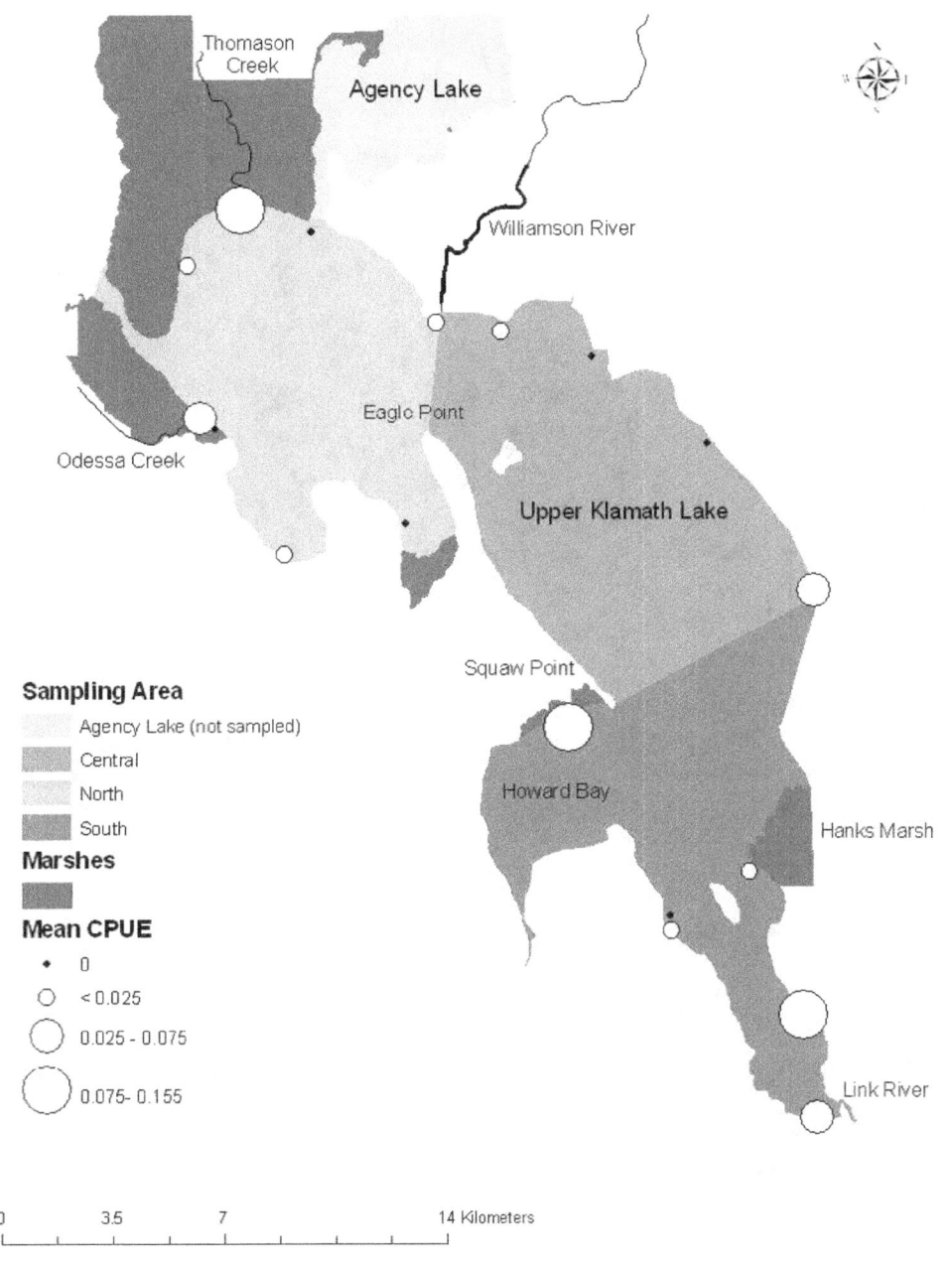

Figure 1. Sampling areas, sampling sites, and mean catch per unit effort (CPUE; fish/hour) for age-1 suckers caught in overnight trap net sets between April 2 and May 29, 2007, in Upper Klamath Lake, Oregon. Locations of major wetlands adjacent to the lake and locations of major tributaries also are shown. Each week a total of six overnight trap nets were set at three sites throughout the lake. One net at each site was set 50 m from shore and the other at 200 m from shore.

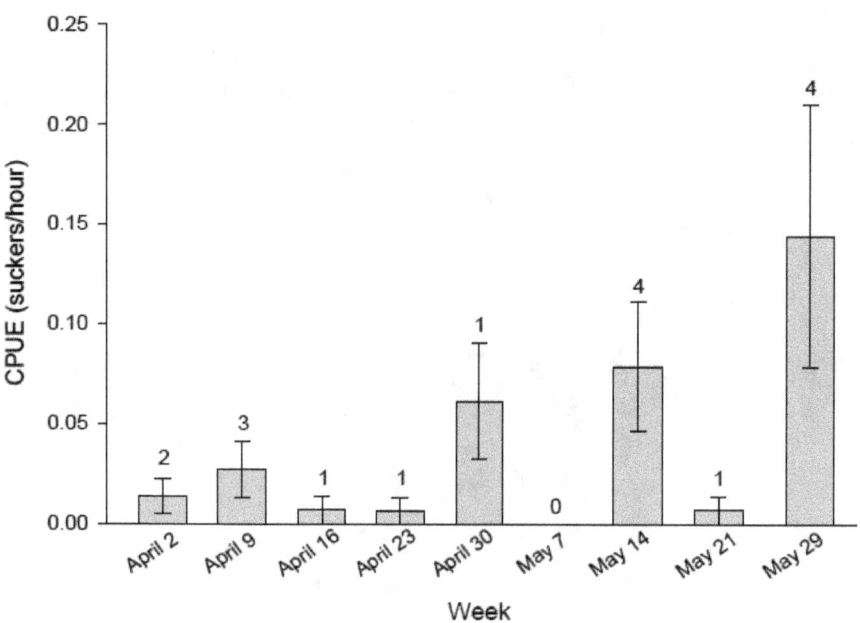

Figure 2. Mean daily catch per unit effort (CPUE; suckers/ hour) ± SE for age-1 suckers captured by trap nets between April 2 and May 29, 2007, in Upper Klamath Lake, Oregon. Each week a total of six overnight trap nets were set at three sites throughout the lake. One net at each site was set 50 m from shore and the other at 200 m from shore. The numbers of nets that caught at least one sucker each week are given.

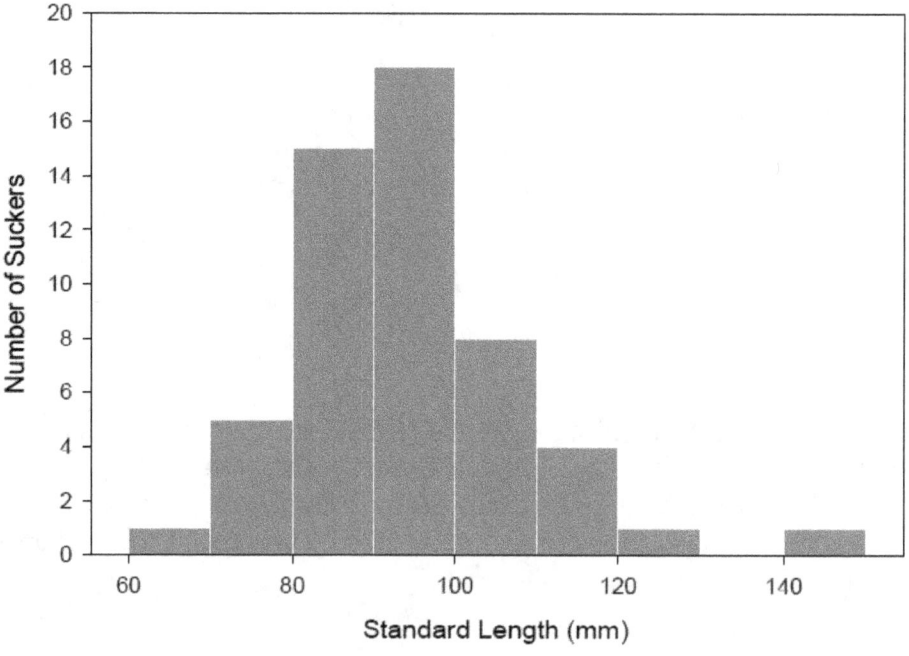

Figure 3. Length frequency distribution for suckers caught in trap nets set in Upper Klamath Lake, Oregon, between April 2 and May 29, 2007.

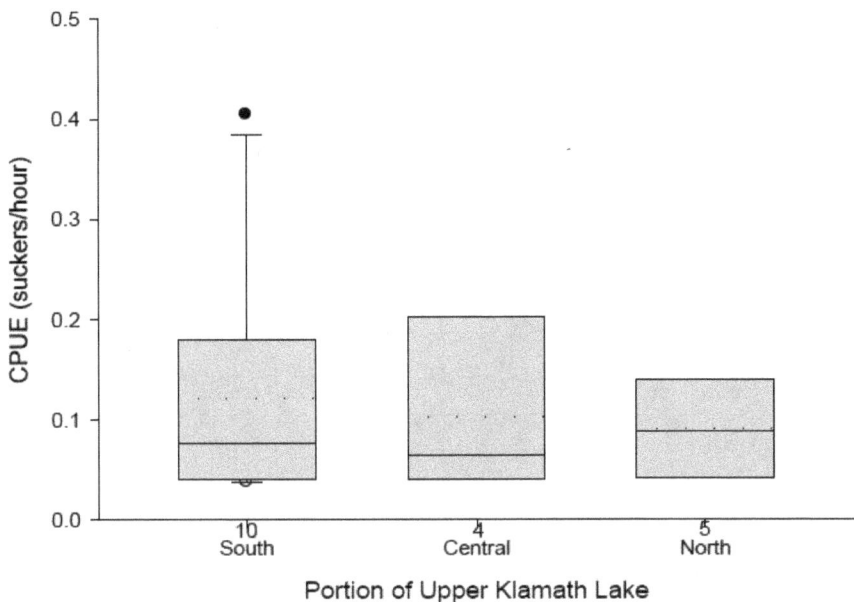

Figure 4. Distribution of catch rates (CPUE; suckers/hour) in trap nets that caught one or more suckers by portion of Upper Klamath Lake, Oregon (see fig. 1), between April 2 and May 29, 2007. Whiskers show 5th and 95th percentiles, boxes encompass 25th and 75th percentiles, dots indicate outliers, solid lines show medians, and dotted lines indicate means. The number of nets in each portion of the lake that caught at least one sucker and were used to create these plots also are given.

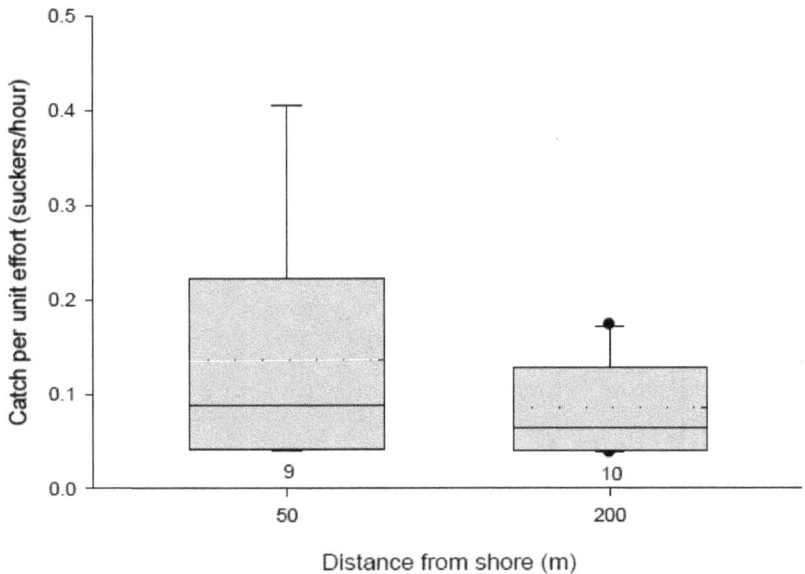

Figure 5. Distribution of catch rates (catch per unit effort; suckers/hour) for trap nets set either 50 m or 200 m from shore in Upper Klamath Lake, Oregon, that caught one or more suckers between April 2 and May 29, 2007 sampling. Whiskers show 5th and 95th percentiles, boxes encompass 25th and 75th percentiles, dots indicate outliers, solid lines show medians, and dotted lines indicate means. The number of nets set at each distance from shore that caught at least one sucker and were used to create these plots also are given.

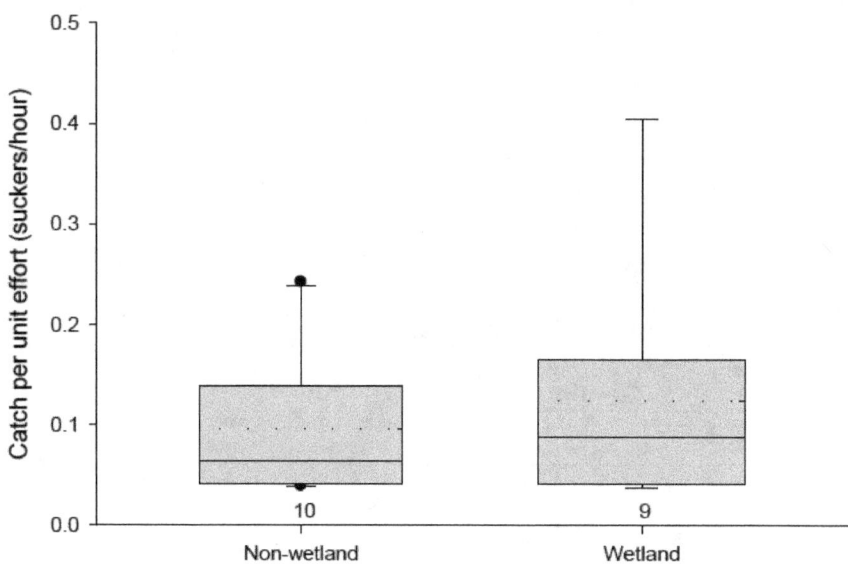

Figure 6. Distribution of catch rates (catch per unit effort; suckers/hour) for trap nets set either adjacent to a wetland (< 250 m) or away from a wetland in Upper Klamath Lake, Oregon, that caught one or more suckers between April 2 and May 29, 2007. Whiskers show 5th and 95th percentiles, boxes encompass 25th and 75th percentiles, dots indicate outliers, solid lines show medians, and dotted lines indicate means. The number of nets set at each distance from shore that caught at least one sucker and were used to create these plots also are given.

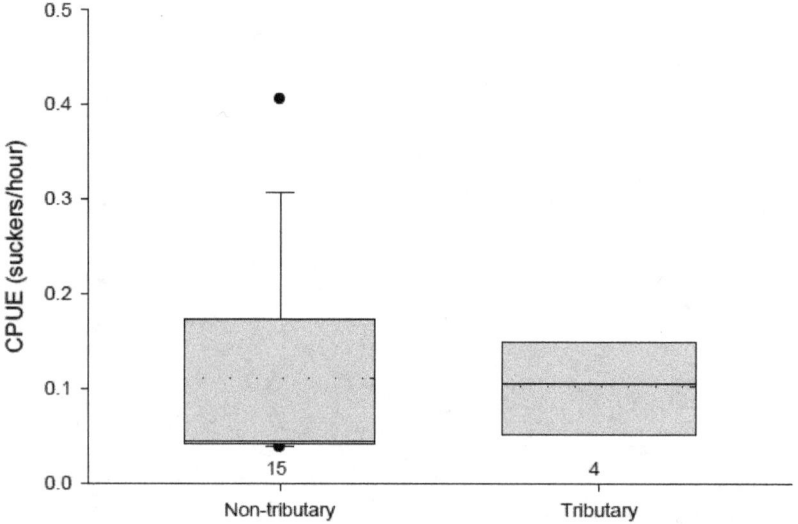

Figure 7. Distribution of catch rates (CPUE; suckers/hour) for trap nets set either adjacent to a tributary mouth or away from a tributary mouth in Upper Klamath Lake, Oregon, that caught one or more suckers, between April 2 and May 29, 2007. Whiskers show 5th and 95th percentiles, boxes encompass 25th and 75th percentiles, dots indicate outliers, solid lines show medians, and dotted lines indicate means. The number of nets set at each distance from shore that caught at least one sucker and were used to create these plots also are given.

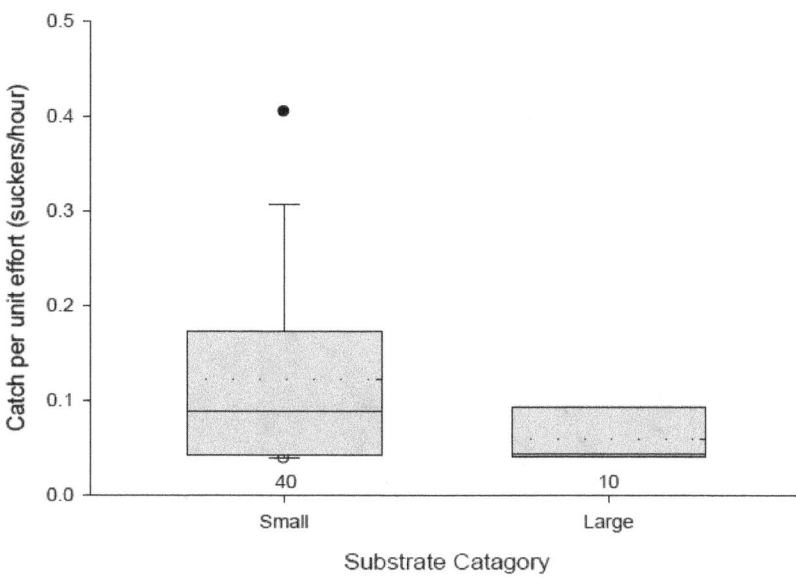

Figure 8. Distribution of catch rates (catch per unit effort; suckers/hour) for trap nets set over small and large substrate in Upper Klamath Lake, Oregon, that caught one or more suckers between April 2 and May 29, 2007. Whiskers show 5th and 95th percentiles, boxes encompass 25th and 75th percentiles, dots indicate outliers, solid lines show medians, and dotted lines indicate means. The number of nets set at each distance from shore that caught at least one sucker and were used to create these plots also are given.

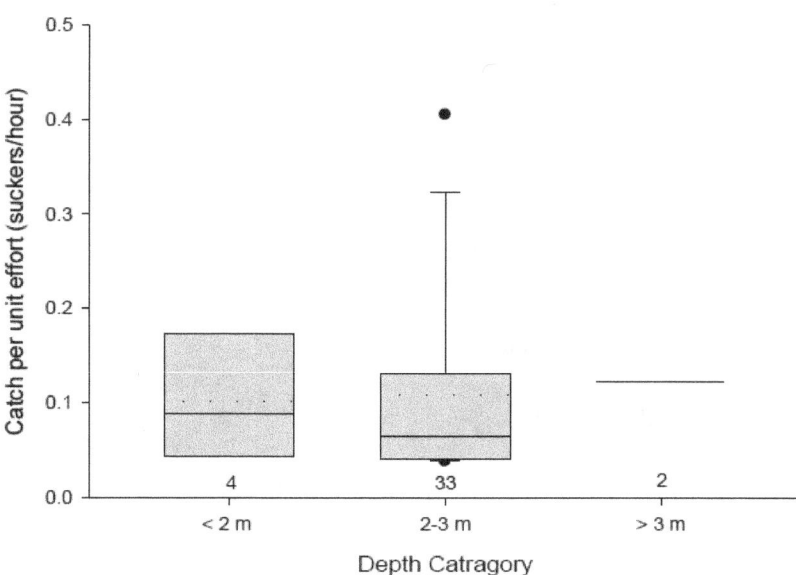

Figure 9. Distribution of catch rates (catch per unit effort; suckers/hour) for trap nets set in three depth categories in Upper Klamath Lake, Oregon, that caught one or more suckers between April 2 and May 29, 2007. Whiskers show 5th and 95th percentiles, boxes encompass 25th and 75th percentiles, dots indicate outliers, solid lines show medians, and dotted lines indicate means. The number of nets set at each distance from shore that caught at least one sucker and were used to create these plots also are given.

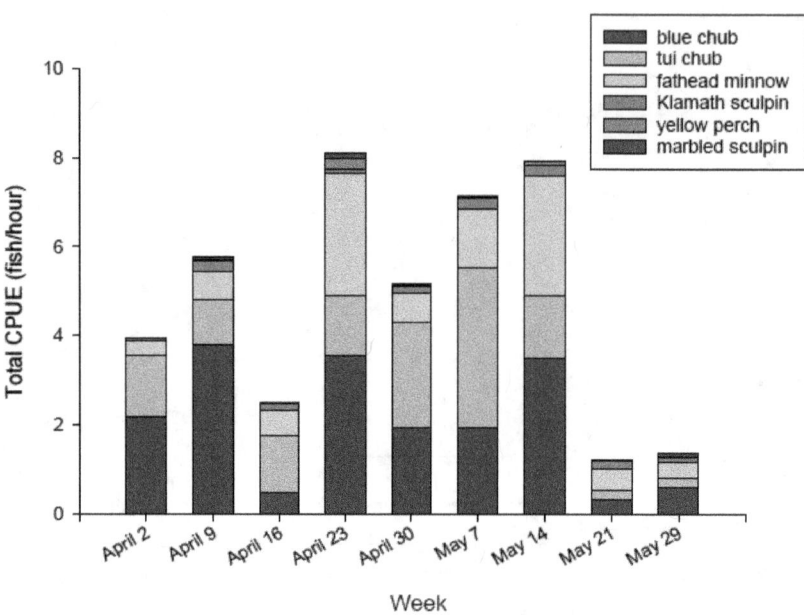

Figure 10. Total catch per unit effort (CPUE; fish/hour) by week for the six most common species captured in trap nets in Upper Klamath Lake between April 2 and May 29, 2007. Each week a total of six overnight trap nets were set at three sites throughout the lake. One net at each site was set 50 m from shore and the other at 200 m from shore.

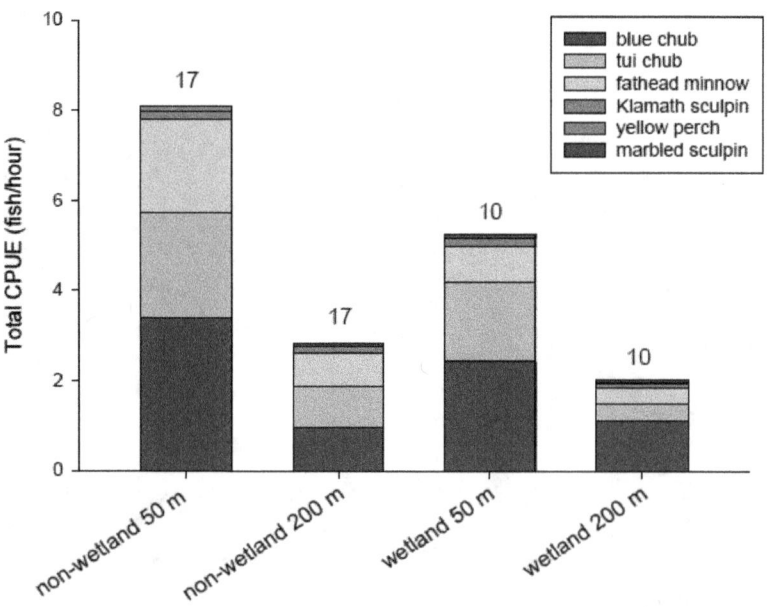

Figure 11. Total catch per unit effort (CPUE; fish/hour) for the six most common species captured in trap nets in Upper Klamath Lake between April 2 and May 29, 2007, by distance from shore (meters) for nets set near (≤ 200 m) or distant (> 200 m) from a wetland. Each week a total of six overnight trap nets were set at thee sites throughout the lake. One net at each site was set 50 m from shore and the other at 200 m from shore. The number of net sets used for each stacked bar plot are given.

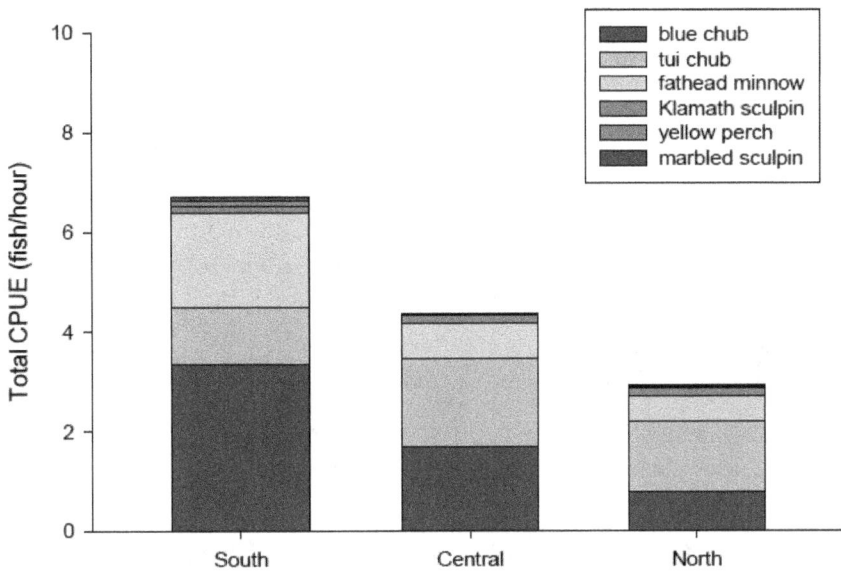

Figure 12. Total catch per unit effort (CPUE; fish/hour) for the six most common species captured in trap nets in Upper Klamath Lake between April 2 and May 29, 2007, by portion of the lake sampled (see fig. 1). The three areas of the lake sampled were: (1) north and west of Eagle Point and the mouth of the Williamson River (North), (2) south and east of Eagle Point and the mouth of the Williamson River and north of Squaw Point and Hagelstein Park (Central), (3) south of Hagelstein Park and Squaw Point including Howard Bay (South; fig. 1). Trap net sets were distributed approximately equally among the three areas (North = 16, Central = 18, South = 20). Each week a total of six overnight trap nets were set at three sites throughout the lake. One net at each site was set 50 m from shore and the other at 200 m from shore.

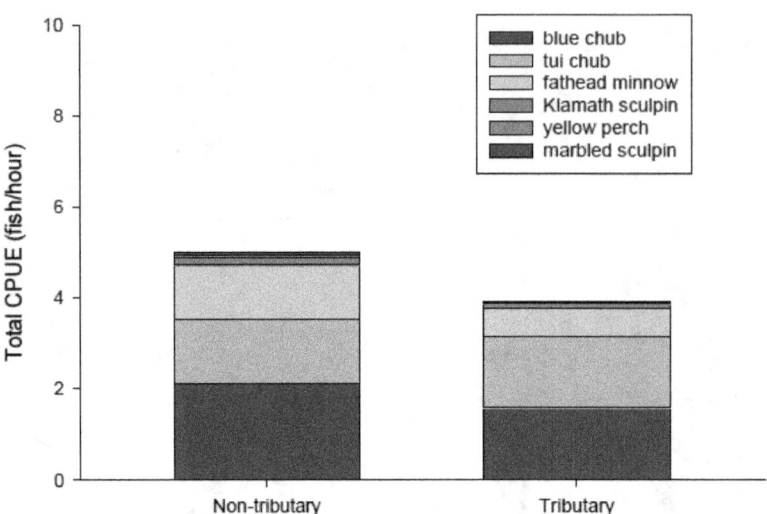

Figure 13. Total catch per unit effort (CPUE; fish/hour) for the six most common species captured in trap nets in Upper Klamath Lake between April 2 and May 29, 2007, for trap nets set near (≤ 200 m) or distant (> 200 m) from a tributary mouth. Each week a total of six overnight trap nets were set at three sites throughout the lake. One net at each site was set 50 m from shore and the other at 200 m from shore. A total of 10 nets were set near tributaries and 44 were set away from tributary mouths.

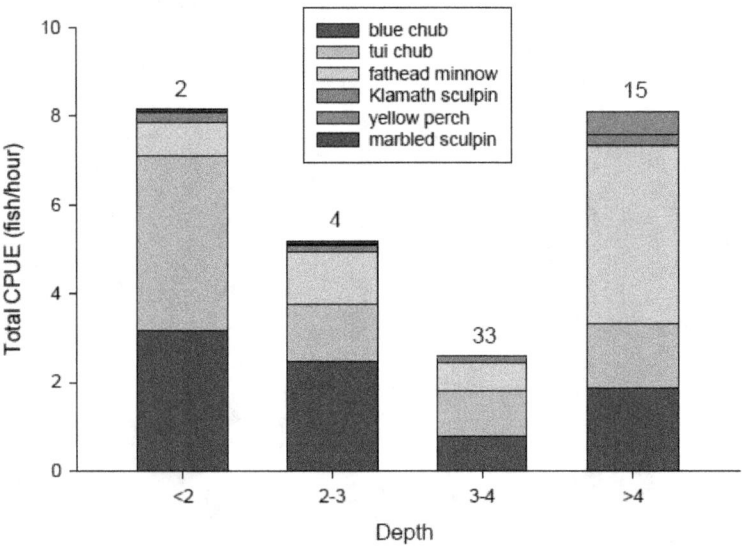

Figure 14. Total catch per unit effort (CPUE; fish/hour) for the six most common species captured in trap nets in Upper Klamath Lake between April 2 and May 29, 2007, by water depth category (in meters). Each week a total of six overnight trap nets were set at three sites throughout the lake. One net at each site was set 50 m from shore and the other at 200 m from shore. The number of nets set in each depth category is given.

18

Chapter 2.—Summer Distribution of Age-0 and Age-1 Suckers in Relation to Environmental Variables in Upper Klamath Lake, Oregon

By Summer M. Burdick and Scott P. VanderKooi, U.S. Geological Survey

Introduction

Rapid declines in catch rates for juvenile endangered Lost River sucker *Deltistes luxatus* and shortnose sucker *Chasmistes brevirostris* and a lack of substantial recruitment into adult sucker populations in recent years suggests that these sucker populations experience high mortality between their first summer and first spawn. Low relative catch rates in Upper Klamath Lake, Oregon, of age-1 compared to age-0 Lost River and shortnose suckers may be due to sampling the wrong environments, poor detection probability, or the true rarity of this age class. Infrequent recruitment into the spawning population suggests suckers experience high mortality between their first summer and first spawn (National Research Council, 2004), which may be exacerbated by diminishing rearing habitat and declining water quality. The causes and rates of mortality can not be adequately assessed, however, without first examining age-dependent catchability and seasonal dynamics in distribution and habitat use of age-0 and age-1 suckers. This is because most methods of assessing mortality depend on the assumptions that all age classes of fish are equally likely to be captured and that a representative sample of individuals from a homogenously distributed population can be obtained (Guy and Brown, 2007).

Although summer age-0 sucker habitat use and distribution is fairly well understood in Upper Klamath Lake (VanderKooi and Buelow, 2003; Terwilliger and others, 2004; Hendrixson and others, 2007a; Hendrixson and others, 2007b; VanderKooi and others, 2007; Burdick and others, 2008a; Burdick and others, 2008b), almost no information exists on the habitat use and distribution of age-1 suckers for the same time of year. Between 2001 and 2006, age-1 and older juvenile suckers were sporadically caught in open water and environments dominated by *Scirpus* spp. (VanderKooi and Buelow, 2003; Hendrixson and others, 2007a; Hendrixson and others, 2007b; VanderKooi and others, 2007). Catch rates between 2001 and 2006 tended to be slightly greater within 200 m of shore than in nets set 400 or 600 m from shore (n = 24; U.S. Geological Survey, unpub. data, 2001–06). Nearshore sampling from 2004 to 2006 indicated that age-1 and older juvenile suckers were approximately equally dispersed in the north (56 percent, n=14) and south (44 percent, n=11) ends of the lake (U.S. Geological Survey, unpub. data, 2001–06). Nearshore to offshore trap net transect surveys at five locations along the eastern shore of Upper Klamath Lake between 2002 and 2006 indicated that age-1 suckers are concentrated around Hagelstein Park and the mouth of the Williamson River in early July (VanderKooi and Buelow, 2003; Hendrixson and others, 2007a; Hendrixson and others, 2007b; VanderKooi and others, 2007). However, all these habitat use and distribution trends are based on very small sample sizes and should be interpreted with extreme caution.

The effects of water quality on age-0 and age-1 sucker distribution are not well understood, but may be a key component in understanding seasonal changes in habitat use. A positive correlation between age-0 sucker catch rates and concentrations of dissolved oxygen (mg/L; DO) was measured in several previous studies (Buettner and Scoppettone, 1990; Terwilliger and others, 2004). Martin and Saiki (1999) determined that concentrations of DO are the most critical factor affecting juvenile Lost River sucker survival in Upper Klamath Lake, which may help explain the association between high concentrations of DO and juvenile sucker catch rates. Lethal pH levels and concentrations of DO for juvenile Lost River and shortnose suckers (Saiki and others, 1999) occur locally in areas of Upper Klamath Lake almost every year (Terwilliger and others, 2004; Wood and others, 2006), and sublethal levels (Loftus, 2001) are common throughout the lake in July and August (Wood and others, 2006). In Upper Klamath Lake, pH and DO are positively correlated as a result of increased photosynthetic activity by massive blooms of *Aphanizomenon flos-aquae* (Wood and others, 2006). Therefore, environments with both low pH and high DO may be unavailable during bloom cycles, forcing juvenile suckers to settle for one or the other. For example, Burdick and others (2008b) reported slightly higher occupancy rates by age-0 suckers at sites with both high pH and DO, rather than at sites with low or moderate pH and high DO.

Differential detection of a species among environments or age classes, often unaccounted for in fisheries research, can lead to biased conclusions about habitat use (MacKenzie, 2005; MacKenzie and others, 2006) or mortality rates. For example, studies that assessed capture efficiency for amphibians and stream-dwelling salmonids determined that gear bias varied among sampling sites and sampling occasions, and was dependent on environmental variables (Bailey and others, 2004; Peterson and others, 2004; Weir and others, 2005). The probability of detecting age-0 suckers in fyke nets set near shore in less than 3 m of water is negatively correlated with depth and positively associated with catch rates in mid to late summer (Burdick and others, 2008b). Failing to account for these variations in detection would cause erroneously low estimates of occupancy in early summer and deeper water.

Our 2007 summer sampling protocol was designed to quantitatively estimate detection probability, distribution, and habitat use of age-0 and age-1 suckers throughout the Upper Klamath Lake. We estimated site-occupancy rates of juvenile suckers in the presence of imperfect detection by sampling sites multiple times simultaneously and using an analysis method described by MacKenzie and others (2006). Our approach allowed us to evaluate the importance of water depth, distance from shore, substrate type, water quality, and month in relation to habitat use and detection probability of age-0 and age-1 suckers. The effectiveness of this relatively new methodology was recently demonstrated for age-0 suckers in nearshore environments in Upper Klamath Lake (Burdick and others, 2008b). The information we present in this chapter regarding summer distribution and habitat use for age-0 and age-1 suckers will help improve sampling design for future research and assist in management of water resources, endangered species, and restoration efforts.

Methods

Collection of Samples

We used a random stratified sampling design to examine age-0 and age-1 sucker summer (early June to mid-September) habitat use in Upper Klamath Lake. We sampled six strata, which included nearshore and offshore strata in each of three areas of Upper Klamath Lake: (1) north and west of Eagle Point and the mouth of the Williamson River, (2) south and east of Eagle Point and the mouth of the Williamson River and north of Squaw Point and Hagelstein Park, and (3) south of Hagelstein Park and Squaw Point including Howard Bay (fig. 1). Sites available for sampling were conceptualized as 2,500-m² cells covering the entire lake. Available nearshore sites consisted of two concentric 50 × 50-m rectangular bands running along the entire shoreline. Offshore sites were considered hexagonal cells at least 100 m from shore.

At each site, we collected three overnight simultaneous trap net samples, using rectangular nets with mouth dimensions of 0.609 × 0.914 m, a 15-m lead, and three internal fykes. Nets were set with mouth openings 120 degrees from each other to avoid interference among nets. At each site in water less than 3 m deep, we confirmed substrate classifications, based on a report by Eilers and Eilers (2007), by probing the bottom of the lake with a PVC pole. The set and pull times, orientation of the net mouth, and lead and mouth depths were recorded for each net. Lead and mouth depths for all three nets at each site were averaged for analysis.

Captured fish were identified to species or lowest practical taxonomic group and counted. Standard length (SL) was taken for all suckers. When catches exceeded 2 to 3 kg, a subsample was taken for all species except juvenile suckers. Prior to subsampling, the presence and absence of each species in the entire sample was recorded in three size bins (small, < 100 mm SL; medium, 100–200 mm SL; and large, ≥ 200 mm SL), and all suckers were measured and removed from the sample. Subsamples were taken by placing the entire sample in a large water-filled tub, thoroughly mixing the contents of the tub, and removing about 30 percent of the original sample weight using a dip net. The total number of each species in the total catch was estimated by extrapolation using the ratio of subsample weight to total weight. Subsample species composition was assumed representative of total catch. Catch per unit effort (CPUE; fish/hour) was calculated for each non-sucker species by dividing the number caught in a net by the number of hours each net was set.

One out of three captured suckers 70 mm SL or less, and 1 out of 10 suckers 70 to 145 mm SL were sacrificed and preserved in 95-percent denatured ethanol for identification to species. We identified juvenile suckers to species in the laboratory with a method developed by Markle and others (2005) using a combination of techniques including vertebrae enumeration, lip morphology, and gill raker counts. The estimated number of each sucker species in a catch was obtained by multiplying the species proportion in the subsample of sacrificed fish by the total number of juvenile suckers caught in the sample. We classified suckers as age-0, age-1, or older based on weekly length frequency plots. Otoliths for a subset of 10 suckers estimated to be age-1 based on length histograms were sent to Oregon State University for ageing.

We used ArcMap 9.2 to associate our sample sites with water-quality stations and mapped substrates. Each sample site was associated with 1 of 17 USGS water-quality monitoring stations located throughout Upper Klamath Lake. The most representative water-quality station, not necessarily the nearest, was selected based on typical summer flow patterns (Wood and others, 2006). At each water-quality station, DO, pH, and temperature (°C) were recorded hourly by the Oregon Water Science Center. Hawth's Analysis Tools (Beyer, 2006) was used to associate each site with substrate as mapped by Eilers and Eilers (2007). Mud, clay, and sand substrates were classified as small, whereas gravel, cobble, rock and boulder substrates were classified as large in our analysis.

Analysis of Data

Development of Models

We estimated habitat use separately for age-0 and age-1 suckers with a suite of occupancy models (MacKenzie and others, 2006) in which we accounted for detection probability concurrently with the probability of habitat use. With three nets at each site, there are $i=8$ possible outcomes and corresponding capture histories (h_i). Capture histories are denoted as a series of 0's and 1's, where 1 indicates that a sucker was captured in a net and a 0 indicates the opposite. A probability function can be written for each capture history by allowing ψ to indicate the probability that a site is occupied by a sucker of age a at the time of sampling, and p to indicate the probability of detecting at least one sucker of age a given the presence of suckers of this age group at a site. Therefore, if at least one sucker in age class a is captured, then the probability statement can be written as follows:

$$\Pr(h_i) = \psi p^{n_1} (1-p)^{n_0},$$

where n_1 is the number of nets at a site that caught suckers in age class a and n_0 is the number of nets that did not catch suckers of that age class. The probability of not capturing any suckers in an age class can be written as:

$$\Pr(h_i) = \psi (1-p)^{n_0} + (1-\psi) \quad .$$

We estimated p and ψ separately for age-0 and age-1 suckers using a maximum likelihood approach in program MARK (White and Burnham, 1999). Based on observed data, Program MARK maximizes the likelihood function:

$$L(p,\psi \mid h_i) = \prod_{i=1}^{s} \Pr(h_i),$$

which is the product of probabilities of all observed encounter histories (h_i).

We used a logit link function to model the effect of covariates on the odds of detection and occupancy. The logit function is defined as:

$$\ln\left(\frac{\theta_i}{1-\theta_i}\right) = \beta_0 + \beta_1 x_{i1} + \ldots + \beta_j x_{ij}$$

where β_j determines the size of the effect of covariates x_j, and θ_i is the parameter of interest (p or ψ).

This method required a number of reasonable assumptions to be made. First, we assumed non-suckers were never erroneously identified as suckers, and that ages were correctly determined. We also assumed detection and presence of age-0 or age-1 suckers was independent among sites and samples. For example, if an age-0 sucker was detected in one net, we assumed at least two more age-0 suckers were available to be captured in the other two nets at the same site.

To model the factors associated with age-0 and age-1 sucker detection probability (p) and habitat use (ψ), we developed a set of *a priori* candidate models based on a literature review and our previous observations. Each candidate model was a mathematical description of a working hypothesis that explained age-0 or age-1 sucker distributions in Upper Klamath Lake. We fit models having only parameters for either p or ψ first. We then fit models in which p and ψ were parameterized. If a variable was hypothesized to affect detection probability or use of an environment, a model was included to incorporate both effects. The biological interpretation for all covariates included as part of the logit submodels are given in table 1.

All models were applied to both age groups, with the exception of a model including a covariate for the presence or absence of fish predators, which was not suitable for age-1 suckers that have few to no fish predators in Upper Klamath Lake. In our most basic candidate models, age-0 or age-1 suckers were considered to be uniformly distributed and equally detectable across all sites. Parameters included in our models described physical environmental characteristics (substrate size, area of lake sampled, and water depth), fish communities (presence of predators and species richness), or water-quality factors (pH, DO, and temperature). Because we did not stratify our sampling by the presence or absence of vegetation, and vegetated environments are relatively rare in Upper Klamath Lake (only 13 percent of sampled sites had any vegetation at all), the presence or absence of vegetation was not included as a variable. We hypothesized that habitat usage would be maximized at some intermediate value of either depth or temperature. We expressed these hypotheses with second-order polynomials in the logit submodels. To ensure that numerical-optimization algorithms could find the correct parameter estimates, all covariate data were scaled to a value between -1 and 1 in program MARK by subtracting the mean of the covariate from the individual value and dividing by the standard deviation (Cooch and White, 2008).

Mean water-quality measurements for DO, pH, and temperature for the week leading up to and including the day of sampling were used as parameters to describe ψ in our models. Water temperature averaged over the duration of the net set was used as a parameter to explain variation in p. We also included stress index covariates for DO and pH based on an equation presented by Loftus (2001). Based on available data, Loftus (2001) determined the concentrations or levels of water-quality parameters likely to initiate physiologically adaptive responses (low-stress thresholds), and at which adverse sublethal effects are likely to occur (high-stress thresholds). The Loftus (2001) stress indices place the effect of water-quality metrics between high- and low-stress thresholds on a scale between 0 and 1. Low-stress thresholds were reached at concentrations of DO of 6 mg/L or pH of 9.00. High-stress thresholds were reached at concentrations of DO of 4 mg/L or pH of 9.75.

Selection of Models

Candidate models were ranked using Akaike's Information Criteria (AIC) adjusted for small sample size (AICc; Burnham and Anderson, 2002). Use of AIC provides a method of ranking models based on their $\log_e$ likelihood with a penalty for the number of parameters to encourage parsimony. When the ratio between the sample size (n) and the number of parameters is less than or equal to 40, Burnham and Anderson (2002) recommend a small sample size adjustment be added to the AIC ranking. Because this adjustment approaches 0 as n becomes large, it is appropriate regardless of sample size; thus we applied the adjustment.

We examined the fit of our most parameterized age-0 and age-1 models, to which all other models in each set were compared, with a bootstrapped estimate of a variance inflation factor $(\hat{c})$. We generated bootstrapped estimates of $\hat{c}$ in Program PRESANCE with 1,000 iterations each for the most parameterized model in each model set. An estimated $\hat{c}$ greater than 1 indicated that either unmodeled heterogeneity or a lack of independence among sites and was used to adjust the variance and AICc rankings. Variance-adjusted rankings are referred to as quasi-AIC ranks (QAICc) in the results section.

Delta QAICc and QAICc normalized weights (w_i) were calculated in program MARK for each model, and used to interpret relative model ranks and calculate average parameter estimates. Normalized weights are calculated by dividing each model weight $\left(\exp\left(\frac{-\Delta AICc}{2} \right) \right)$ by the sum of all model weights in a group of models (Cooch and White, 2008). A confidence set of models was defined as models having a w_i no less than 10 percent of the w_i for the most parsimonious model (Burnham and Anderson, 2002). For comparison between two models, we calculated evidence ratios as the ratio between the two model weights.

Parameter Estimation

To incorporate model uncertainty, we model averaged over all models for each age class to estimate probability of detection (p), habitat use (ψ), β_j from the logit submodels, and the variances associated with these estimates (Burnham and Anderson, 2002; MacKenzie and others, 2006). To estimate $\hat{p}$ and $\hat{\psi}$ given environmental conditions of interest, we back-transformed estimates of β_is, and used the delta method to calculate confidence intervals (Cooch and White, 2008). For models containing polynomial habitat-use submodels, we calculated habitat-use probability curves. To find the point at which these curves were maximized, we took the derivative, set it equal to 0, and solved for the parameter estimate.

Models that rank high using AIC identify which parameters are important for explaining variation in habitat use, but do not indicate the direction or magnitude of parameter effects. Odds ratios indicate that the direction and magnitude of parameter effects and allow us to understand how environmental and community variables affect habitat use and detection. To examine the effects of model parameters on habitat use and detection, we calculated odds ratios and their confidence limits for all $\hat{p}$ and $\hat{\psi}$ logit submodel variables contained in at least one monomial model in each confidence set of models (MacKenzie and others, 2006). Odds ratios for a single unit of change were calculated as e^{β_i}, and standard errors for odds ratios were estimated as:

$$ SE(\beta_i) = \sqrt{\frac{e^{\beta_i}}{\left(1 - e^{\beta_i}\right)} \mathrm{var}(\beta_i)} . $$

We limited our reporting of confidence bands to the interval between 0 and 1 because higher and lower values have no biological meaning.

We used two approaches to examine species interactions. Species richness, calculated as the total number of non-sucker species caught at a site, was included as a covariate in a logit submodel for ψ for each age group. The presence of predators was used as a covariate to model heterogeneity in ψ for age-0 suckers. Potential predators were considered to be individual fish from of any of the following species more than 100 mm SL: yellow perch, pumpkinseed, brown bullhead, and rainbow trout.

Results of Data Collection and Analysis

We set three overnight net sets at each of 354 sites in six strata including nearshore and offshore strata in the northern, central, and southern areas of the lake (fig. 1). Three nets failed, two due to loosely tied cod ends and one due to disturbance. Site depths averaged 2.76 m and ranged from 0.42 m to 11.05 m. Median depths at sample sites were similar between nearshore and offshore environments (Mann-Whitney test; $p = 0.03$). The majority of sites were set over mud (74 percent), followed by boulder substrates (15 percent). Less than 3 percent of sites had sand, clay, gravel, cobble, or rock substrate. All together, 79 percent of sites had small substrate and 21 percent had large substrates as defined in the methods section of this chapter.

Average water-quality characteristics over 7 days or the duration of net sets were mostly within the range of conditions considered non-stressful to suckers (Loftus, 2001). The 7-day mean concentration of DO ranged from 2.1 to 12.9 mg/L with a median of 8.5 mg/L. Conversely, concentrations of DO averaged over the duration of a net set indicated much greater short-term swings, and ranged from 0.4 to 14.1 mg/L. Dissolved oxygen averaged over 7 days or over the duration of a net set decreased below the high-stress threshold (4 mg/L) for suckers at only 7 percent of sites but decreased below the low-stress threshold for suckers (6 mg/L) at 20 percent and 23 percent of sites, respectively. The 7-day mean levels of pH ranged from 4.7 to 10.3 and had a median of 9.5. The 7-day mean levels of pH exceeded the low-stress threshold for suckers (9.00) at 79 percent of sites and the high-stress threshold (9.75) at 20 percent of sites. The low-stress threshold for temperature (25 °C) was never exceeded by the 7-day mean temperature calculations and was exceeded by the mean temperature calculated for the duration of the net sets on only two occasions. Mean temperature calculated for the net set duration ranged from 16.4 and 25.8 °C and had a median of 20.5 °C. Both measures of temperature peaked between July 16 and August 2 (fig. 2).

With the exception of two suckers less than 45 mm SL captured on June 12 and June 28, age-0 suckers began recruiting to our nets during the week of July 9 between 34 and 44 mm SL. Age-1 suckers were captured in our nets in all 14 weeks of sampling and ranged in size from 74 to 110 mm SL the week of June 11, and 130 to 150 mm SL the last week of sampling (September 10). Age-0 sucker catches peaked the week of August 5 (fig. 3), whereas age-1 sucker catches were relatively high until the week of July 16, but rapidly declined each week for the rest of the sampling season (fig. 3). We captured age-0 suckers in 49.4 percent of nets at 26.5 percent of sites and age-1 suckers in 37.2 percent of nets at 27.4 percent of sites. The percentage of nets to catch at least one age-0 sucker was greatest during the week of August 5 (fig. 3), and the percentage of nets to catch at least one age-1 sucker was greatest during the week of July 2 (fig. 3).

Most of the 363 sacrificed age-0 suckers were identified as Lost River suckers (53.2 percent). The second largest portion of sacrificed age-0 suckers was identified as shortnose suckers (42.1 percent). Only 0.6 percent of sacrificed age-0 suckers were identified as Klamath largescale suckers and 4.1 percent were unidentifiable with our methodology. In contrast, most of the 22 sacrificed age-1 suckers were identified as shortnose (72.7 percent). Lost River, Klamath largescale, and suckers that were unidentifiable with our methodology each made up only 9.1 percent of all sacrificed age-1 suckers. We measured a shift in the ratio of shortnose suckers to Lost River suckers in our sacrificed age-0 sucker samples through time. From the week of July 9 to September 3, this ratio increased from 1:3 to 2.67:1. In the final week of sampling (September 10), this ratio dipped only slightly to 2.38:1.

Deformed opercles and anchorworms *Lernaea* spp. were commonly observed on sacrificed age-0 suckers but no deformities and very few anchorworms were found on sacrificed age-1 suckers. A total of 27 percent of sacrificed age-0 Lost River suckers had at least one severely deformed opercle and 36 percent of these had both opercles deformed. In contrast, only 3 percent of sacrificed age-0 shortnose suckers had at least one severely deformed opercle, and 20 percent of these had two deformed opercles. Anchorworms were found on a high percentage of sacrificed age-0 Lost River suckers (45 percent) and shortnose suckers (38 percent). Anchorworms, however, were not abundant when they were present. The number of anchorworms per sucker ranged from one to nine, but 95 percent of sacrificed age-0 suckers with anchorworms had fewer than three.

An examination of CPUE by water depth revealed different patterns for age-0 and age-1 suckers, but patterns generally were similar between Lost River and shortnose suckers of the same age group (fig. 4). Mean catch rates of age-0 suckers combined over all species were greatest in nets set in 1 to 2 m of water and lowest in nets set at depths of 4 m or greater. Catch rates were highest for age-0 suckers in 1 to 2 m of water for shortnose suckers and in 2 to 3 m of water for Lost River suckers. For age-1 suckers, mean CPUE gradually increased with depth to a peak in the 4 to 5 m category. Due to insufficient numbers of sacrificed age-1 suckers that were identified to species, a species-specific analysis of CPUE by depth was not possible.

Non-sucker fish species were caught at high rates and had wide spatial distributions. The number of species caught at a site ranged from 0 to 10 with a mean of 6.2. Calculated CPUE for all non-sucker species in each trap net ranged from 0 to 404 fish/hour, but was less than 24 fish/hour in 95 percent of nets. Seasonal peaks in catch rates of non-sucker species were not as pronounced as they were for juvenile suckers (fig. 5). Mean weekly CPUE for fathead minnow and tui chub were greatest during the week of July 23, 2 weeks before age-0 sucker catch rates peaked (fig. 3). However, peak catch rates for Upper Klamath marbled sculpin and blue chub occurred after the peak in age-0 sucker catches. Of all non-sucker species caught, 98 percent were less than 200 mm SL and 75 percent were less than 100 mm SL.

Juvenile blue chub, juvenile tui chub, fathead minnow, and Klamath Lake sculpin *Cottus princeps* were each captured in 75 percent or more of all nets set and at 91 percent or more of all sites (fig. 5). Upper Klamath marbled sculpin, which were captured at 78 percent of sites (54 percent or nets), and yellow perch, captured at 67 percent of sites (47 percent of nets) also were widely distributed. Brown bullhead, pumpkinseed, lamprey *Lampetra* spp., and slender sculpin *C. tennuis* were captured much less frequently and were only present in our nets at 16 to 34 percent of sites. The least common species in our catches were largemouth bass *Micropterus salmoides*, Klamath speckled dace *Rhinichthys osculus klamathensis*, and Klamath redband trout, which were captured at 1 percent or fewer sites.

Results of Occupancy Analysis

Age-0 Sucker Habitat Use

Our global model had 25 parameters and fit the age-0 dataset very well ($\hat{c}$ = 0.98; table 2). Given that $\hat{c}$ was less than 1, we did not adjust the variance in our age-0 models. All other candidate models had lower AIC values and therefore were considered better than the full model when parsimony was taken into account (table 2).

AIC model rankings indicate that age-0 sucker habitat use was most affected by water temperature (table 2). The top two models contained a parameter for temperature in the habitat use logit submodel and jointly carried 99.9 percent of the model weights. Fit statistics indicated that temperature was at least 18 orders of magnitude better at explaining heterogeneity in habitat use than any other parameter. Model averaged estimates of water temperature effects indicate that age-0 sucker habitat use is maximized at 23.3 °C (fig. 6). We estimate the probability of an age-0 sucker occupying a habitat at this temperature to be 0.66, but confidence intervals include 0 and 1. Therefore, this result should be interpreted as insignificant.

A simple polynomial depth model (model 0-6; table 2) ranked poorly compared to temperature models but was supported by an evidence ratio of 632:1 when compared to the null model. This simple depth effect (model 0-6) was supported by an evidence ratio of 44:1 over a depth-by-month interaction effect (model 0-12). Age-0 sucker habitat use was maximized at a depth of 2.4 m over the course of the sampling season (fig. 7). The probability that a randomly selected site with this depth was occupied by an age-0 sucker during the summer of 2007 was 0.31. Confidence intervals on this estimate, however, spanned 0 and 1 over all depths and this result should be interpreted as insignificant.

The probability of occupancy for age-0 suckers varied by month but not by distance from shore. The effect of a month on occupancy (model 0-13) is supported by an evidence ratio of 47:1 over a model with only a distance from shore effect (model 0-22), and 98:1 over a model with a distance from shore-by-month interaction (model 35; table 2). The estimated portion of used sites ranged from a low of 0 in nearshore area in September, to a high of 73.1 percent (CI = 15–100 percent) in offshore area in July (fig. 8).

Compared to temperature, concentrations of DO and pH poorly explained heterogeneity in habitat use. When considered in conjunction with a homogeneous detection probability, the stress index for pH (model 0-11) was supported with an evidence ratio of 40:1 over the no-effects model (model 0-23). However, a model containing a 7-day average pH (model 0-29) fit the data less well than the no-effects model. The 7-day average DO concentration (model 0-16) explained the variation in the age-0 sucker habitat use 4.3 times better than the no-effects model (model 0-23), and 1.7 times better than the stress index for DO (model 0-18). Estimated odds ratios indicate that age-0 suckers were 2.6 (CI = 1.3 to 5.9) times more likely to use a site with a pH stress index of 1 (pH ≥ 9.75) than of 0 (pH ≤ 9.00) and 1.9 (CI = 1.0-3.9) times more likely to use habitats that have a DO stress index of 1 (DO ≤ 4 mg/L) than of 0 (DO ≥ 6 mg/L).

The presence and relative abundance of non-sucker species was a fair predictor of age-0 sucker presence at sites throughout Upper Klamath Lake. An association between predators and the presence of age-0 suckers (model 0-3) was supported with an evidence ratio of 194,950:1 over the no-effects model (model 0-23) and was 2.5 times better at explaining the variation in habitat use than species richness (model 0-4). Odds ratios indicate that age-0 suckers were 3.7 (CI = 2.2 to 6.1) times more likely to be present at a site where at least one potential predator was detected. Additionally age-0 suckers were 1.5 (CI = 1.2 to 1.8) times more likely to be present for every additional non-sucker species detected at a site.

An overall north-to-south migration of age-0 suckers between June and September was not supported by our models. A month-by-area interaction effect was included in several of the habitat use logit submodels to examine the possibility of directed movement among areas. All models that included this effect ranked very low, indicating a directed movement was unlikely. For example, the no-effects model (model 0-23) fit the data 37,974 times better than model 0-39, which incorporated a month-by-area interaction in the habitat use submodel and no additional parameters in the detection submodel (table 2). Additionally, fit statistics indicated that the top model in the age-0 data set was 28 orders of magnitude better at explaining the data than model 0-39.

Age-0 Sucker Detection Probability

AIC model rankings indicate that detection probability was not strongly affected by water temperature (table 2). The top ranked model contained a parameter for temperature in the detection logit submodel, but was only 1.8 times better at explaining variation in the data than the second-ranked model, which had no submodel parameters for detection. A temperature effect on detection probability was only slightly supported by an evidence ratio of 1:1.5 between the no-effects model (model 0-23) and model 0-21, which has a parameter for temperature in the detection logit submodel. Odds ratios indicated that age-0 suckers were only 1.2 (CI = 1.0–1.4) times more likely to be detected given their presence at a site for every 1°C decrease in temperature averaged over the duration of a net set.

Our results indicate that distance from shore had little to no effect on age-0 sucker detection probability. A distance from shore effect on detection probability was supported by model 0-19, which explained the variation in the data 1.9 times better than the no-effects model (0-23; table 2). Odds ratios indicated that age-0 suckers were 1.5 (CI = 0.8–2.7) times more likely to be detected in offshore environments than nearshore environments given their presence at a site. Given that the confidence interval for this estimate overlaps 1, it should be interpreted as non-significant.

The age-1 sucker data fit the most parameterized model well, but was slightly over dispersed ($\hat{c}$ = 1.24). Therefore, we adjusted the variance in each age-1 sucker model by $\hat{c}$. All other candidate models had lower QAICc values and as a result were considered better than the full model when parsimony and over dispersion were taken into account (table 3). There were 11 models in our confidence set with normalized weights (w_i) ranging from 0.026 to 0.157. The confidence set of models indicated that the primary factors affecting age-1 habitat use were month, distance from shore, and depth. Substrate also was represented in the confidence set of models, but ranked lower than other models, indicating it may have a minor role in determining age-1 habitat use.

An interaction between month and distance from shore is not strongly supported given that the most parsimonious age-1 sucker model had both month and distance from shore effects on habitat use, and fit the data set 1.5 times better than a model including the interaction between these two parameters. Nevertheless, there is a slight trend in odds ratios over time that suggest age-1 suckers used a higher portion of nearshore than offshore areas in June and July, but more offshore than nearshore areas in August and September (fig. 9). The estimated portion of nearshore lake environments used by age-1 suckers ranged from a high of 84.0 percent (CI = 8.7–100.0 percent) in June to a low of 15.0 percent (CI = 0.0–100.0 percent) in September. The portion of offshore lake environments used by age-1 suckers ranged from a high of 70.5 percent (CI = 0.0–100.0 percent) in offshore environments in July to a low of 35.1 percent (CI = 0.0–100.0 percent) in September (fig. 10).

Water depth was an important factor in explaining age-1 sucker habitat use, and depth preferences for this age group did not change by month. Models containing a second-order polynomial for depth in the habitat use logit submodel carried a total of 36.6 percent of all model weights compared to models with a depth-by-month interaction, which carried 24.6 percent of model weights. In addition, models in which month and water depth were considered additive effects out-performed models with month-by-depth interaction terms when all other parameters were similar (table 3). The probability of age-1 sucker occupancy was maximized (max = 0.59) at 4.5 m (fig. 11). However, confidence intervals encompassed 0 and 1 at all depths, suggesting these results should be interpreted as preliminary trends that need to be validated with future research.

Age-1 sucker habitat use was somewhat associated with the presence of larger substrates. Models with a substrate parameter in the habitat use logit submodel carried a total of 9.6 percent of the model weights. A model with only a substrate effect on occupancy (model 1-7) out performed the no-effects model (1-27) with an evidence ratio of 91:1. Odds ratios indicated that age-1 suckers were 2.8 (CI = 1.0–8.0) times more likely to use habitat with large substrate (gravel, cobble, boulder, and rock) than small substrate (sand, mud, and clay) over the course of the sampling season. However, substrate effects may be confounded with depth, given that most large substrate in Upper Klamath Lake is located along the western shore, where the lake is the deepest.

AIC model ranks indicate that water-quality parameters, as they were applied, were relatively poor predictors of age-1 sucker habitat use when compared to other physical habitat parameters. However, models with parameters for temperature and DO concentration fit the data better than the no-effects model (1-27). For example, we calculated an evidence ratio of 1:33 for the top model (1-1) compared to model 1-18, which used a second-order polynomial to describe temperature effects on habitat use (table 3). However, the evidence ratio between model 1-18 and the no-effect model (1-27) is 8:1. Model 1-19, which used the DO stress index to explain habitat use, had an evidence ratio of 1:39 when compared to the most parsimonious model (1-1), but 4:1 when compared to the 7-day mean DO (1-25; table 3). The odds ratio indicates that age-1 suckers are 3.5 (CI = 1.2–10.2) times more likely to use environments with a DO stress index of 0 (DO ≥ 6 mg/L) than with a DO stress index of 1 (DO ≤ 4 mg/L).

We did not detect directed movement of age-1 suckers between June and September among the areas of the lake we examined in our analysis. A month-by-area interaction effect was included in several of the habitat use logit submodels to examine the possibility of directed movement among areas. All models that included this effect ranked very low, indicating a directed movement was unlikely. The no-effects model (1-27) fit the data 28,809:1 times better than model 1-38, which incorporated a month-by-area interaction in the habitat use submodel and no additional parameters in the detection submodel.

Age-1 Sucker Detection Probability

The probability of detecting an age-1 sucker in trap nets was related to distance from shore, substrate, and cover. Models containing a distance from shore effect on detection probability all had lower QAICc values (better ranks) than models with no distance from shore effect on detection when all other parameters were the same. The same was true for substrate and cover effects on detection, but was not always true for models with a depth effect on detection. Odds ratios indicated that age-1 suckers were 3.0 (CI = 1.2–7.7) times more likely to be caught when present in a nearshore site than when present in an offshore site, and 2.3 (CI = 1.1–4.7) times more likely to be detected at sites with large substrate than small substrate.

Distribution of Suckers and Relation to Environmental Variables

Our approach to data analysis allowed us to separate true absences of suckers from false absences caused by incomplete detection, which can be a substantial problem in fisheries (Bayley and Peterson, 2001; Peterson and others, 2004). This method gave us greater confidence that our results were unbiased and accurately represents habitat usage by age-0 and age-1 suckers. Additionally, we were able to rank the importance of environmental variables and estimate the magnitude of influence these variables had on habitat usage. By testing similar model sets for both age-0 and age-1 suckers, we were able to compare and contrast habitat use between these two age classes of suckers.

Major violations of assumptions were unlikely to have occurred in our study. The assumptions that no fish were falsely identified as suckers or assigned a false age classification were supported by subsamples that were preserved and later identified to species. In subsamples, 100 percent of fish identified as suckers in the field were verified as members of the *Catostomidae* family in the laboratory. Additionally, ages were confirmed for 10 suckers suspected to be a 1-year old using otoliths (M. Terwilliger, Oregon State University, unpub. data, 2007). Our use of passive sampling gear ensured that detections were independent among sites sampled on the same day. Forty-two sampling locations were visited twice and considered separate sites in our analysis. This could cause a violation of the independent sample sites assumption, especially if juvenile suckers had a tendency to remain in one location. However, estimated $\hat{c}$ values of 0.98 for age-0 data and 1.24 for age-1 data suggest that the site independence assumption was violated rarely, if at all.

Our results indicate that age-0 suckers within Upper Klamath Lake primarily are habitat generalists, whereas age-1 sucker habitat use varied slightly with water depth, distance from shore, and type of substrate. Low model selection uncertainty in the age-0 sucker model set strengthens conclusions about the broad range of environments used by this age class of suckers within Upper Klamath Lake. However, results for age-1 suckers should be interpreted with caution due to high model selection uncertainty for this age class. Some of the uncertainty in our results may be attributed to our inability to identify all suckers to species with our chosen method, which prevented a species-specific analysis.

Age-0 sucker habitat use increased from June to July and decreased from August to September following the trend in catch rates (figs. 3 and 8). In comparison, age-1 suckers used less overall available lake area (fig. 9) and were less abundant in our catches each month from June to September (fig. 3). The increase in habitat use by age-0 suckers probably is an artifact of recruitment to our gear. The decline in the portion of overall area used throughout the later one-half of the summer by age-0 suckers, and throughout the whole sampling season for age-1 suckers, may be the result of emigration from the lake, mortality, or a tendency to cluster into fewer available lake environments as the lake level declines. However, a directed emigration out of the lake for either age group was not supported by models designed to test this hypothesis. For both age groups, decline in abundance due to mortality or emigration rather than clustering in fewer available lake environments is supported by a general decrease in our catch rates beginning in early August for age-0 suckers and early July for age-1 suckers. These results are corroborated by Burdick and others (2008b), who determined that when more age-0 suckers are present, there is an increase in occupied areas of the lake instead of increased fish densities in selected areas.

AIC rankings indicate that temperature was correlated with age-0 sucker habitat, but standard errors for parameter estimates were large and confidence intervals encompassed 0 and 1 over the entire range of temperatures measured. This lack of precision suggests that water temperature, while better than other parameters, poorly explained heterogeneity in age-0 sucker habitat use. Water temperature values used in our analysis were 7-day means estimated from remote stations, and may have been too imprecise to model the relation with occupancy. Another possibility is that seasonal trends in abundance of age-0 suckers may have been loosely correlated with water temperature, and may have affected the portion of lake environments occupied. Some support for this prospect may be garnered from the comparison of the seasonal peak in mean weekly age-0 sucker CPUE during the week of July 30 (fig. 3) to the seasonal peak in mean weekly water temperatures 1 week later (fig. 4). A higher abundance of age-0 suckers in our catches in July and August (fig. 3) also corresponds with higher occupancy probabilities for this age class (fig. 8).

Age-0 suckers were slightly more likely to use offshore rather than nearshore environments in June and September than in July or August. On the contrary, age-1 suckers were slightly more likely to be found in nearshore than offshore environments in June and July, but in more offshore than nearshore sites in August and September. The slightly higher probability for age-0 suckers to occupy offshore environments in June may be due to earlier recruitment of Lost River suckers, which are thought to use habitats farther from shore than shortnose suckers (D. Markle, Oregon State University, oral commun., 2007). Another explanation is that age-0 suckers move offshore in mid-summer, following an ontogenetic shift in diet (Markle and Clauson, 2006). However, by that rationale, offshore environments would have been occupied at higher rates starting in July, not in September. For both age classes, the slight tendency to move offshore later in the summer may be an artifact of this age class selecting habitat based on another correlated variable, such as depth. Large standard errors for occupancy probabilities (figs. 8 and 9), however, cause uncertainty about differential use of near and offshore environments. Furthermore, models in which sites were grouped into either nearshore or offshore categories ranked low for age-0 suckers, causing additional uncertainty about the relation between distance from shore and habitat use by this age class.

A lack of support for models with a month-by-depth interaction for both age groups indicates that there was not a substantial change in the optimal depth used by either age class in 2007. This is in contrast with Burdick and others (2008b), who showed age-0 suckers used shallow water environments in mid to late July and late August to early September, but exhibited no depth preference during early to mid August in 2004 and 2005. The difference in seasonal depth use presented in these two studies could be due to inter-annual variation, differences in sampling protocol, or different analytical methods. It is unlikely that the depth-by-month interaction went undetected in 2007 due to a lack of statistical power because sample sizes were large in both studies (2007, n = 354; 2004–05, n = 427). Burdick and others (2008b) used a linear model to examine depth rather than the polynomial model used in this study. In this analysis, we examined an additive depth-and-month model and a depth-by-month interaction model, which allowed us to make stronger inferences about how the combination of these variables affected habitat use. The difference between models used in these two studies may partly explain the contrasting results. We believe the analysis presented in this report is an improvement on the previous analysis presented by Burdick and others (2008b).

This study provides some evidence that age-0 suckers were more likely to use shallow water environments, whereas age-1 suckers were more likely to use deeper environments during summer months (fig. 7). Large standard errors for occupancy probabilities cause uncertainty about optimal depth ranges used by both age classes. However, high catch rates of age-0 suckers in nets set in water 1 to 2 m deep and of age-1 suckers in nets set at depths of 4 to 5 m corroborate the findings of the occupancy analysis (fig. 4). Furthermore, depth models ranked low for age-0 suckers, causing additional uncertainty about the relation between depth and occupancy for this age class. Nevertheless, our results are consistent with those of other studies that reported age-0 suckers using shallower environments within sampling ranges (Buettner and Scoppettone, 1990; Burdick and others, 2008b). The range of depths sampled in our present study was wider than in previous studies and indicated that occupancy was maximized at 2.4 m deep for age-0 suckers, whereas Buettner and Scoppettone (1990) reported age-0 suckers primarily were found in water less than 0.5 m deep.

The optimal summer depth indicated by our models for age-1 suckers (4.4 m) was consistent with measured summer depth selection by adult Lost River and shortnose suckers, which primarily use areas greater than 3 m deep (Banish and others, 2009). Age-1 suckers used slightly deeper environments between June and September than in April and May (Chapter 1). Possible explanations for this seasonal shift in depth selection include increased food availability in deeper water in summer than in spring, interactions with other species, or changes in water chemistry or temperature. However, none of these explanations have been investigated and little evidence exists to support them.

The availability of habitats in depth ranges most used by juvenile suckers depends on the lake surface elevation, which changes in response to annual precipitation, irrigation diversions, and downstream releases over the Link River Dam. The Bureau of Reclamation Klamath Project regulates irrigation allocations and downstream releases to maintain a lake-surface elevation within the target range of 4,137.5 ft (1,261.1 m), and 4,142.2 ft (1,262.5 m). The availability of habitats with at least a 30-percent chance of being occupied by age-1 suckers between June and September based on depth (2.4 to 6.5 m) declines rapidly with lake-surface elevation (fig. 10). On the contrary, age-0 suckers use shallow environments that are widely available at all lake elevations under present and proposed management plans.

Our analysis indicates that age-1 suckers were slightly more likely to be found in the presence of larger substrates, but did not imply an effect of substrate size on age-0 sucker habitat use. These results do not necessarily contradict the suggestion by Burdick and others (2008b)or Buettner and Scoppettone (1990) that age-0 suckers are associated with small substrates such as sand and mud. As is true in the present study for age-0 suckers, the trends reported in these previous two studies did not carry the support of statistical significance or another quantitative metric. Therefore, a failure to detect an effect of substrate size on age-0 sucker habitat use in our analysis given a similar underlying truth is possible. Most of substrate in the large size class is composed of boulders (Eilers and Eilers, 2007), and the association of age-1 suckers with large substrate may be due to the cover provided in the interstitial spaces. Another possibility is that the effects of water depth are confounded with substrate size given that most large substrates are located along the western shore in or near deeper water.

We were unable to detect effects of pH levels or concentrations of DO on site occupancy, likely because data were insufficient or the range of parameters was too small to produce an effect. Water-quality conditions at our sample sites generally were within the acceptable range for juvenile suckers, and extremes were rare. Relatively narrow ranges in pH levels and concentrations of DO may have limited our ability to detect significant effects of these parameters on age-0 and age-1 sucker habitat use. Our spatial and temporal resolution also may have been too coarse to detect changes in habitat use in response to local changes in water quality. Burdick and others (2008b) similarly reported a lack of response in occupancy rates to water-quality conditions by age-0 suckers in 2004 and 2005. However, others have reported lower catch rates of juvenile suckers when concentrations of DO were low (Buettner and Scoppettone, 1990; Terwilliger and others, 2004). The difference between occupancy studies and other studies that looked at catch rates may suggest that low concentrations of DO reduce the number of fish in an area, but do not exclude them completely.

The presence of age-0 suckers was correlated with high species richness and the presence of potential predators, whereas age-1 sucker presence was not correlated with species richness. This pattern was unexpected and the underling mechanism is unclear. The most probable cause is age-0 suckers use environments similar to those used by many other species of fish in the lake. However, a more in-depth study on inter-species interactions may reveal a more direct mechanism and should be considered in future studies.

The underlying mechanisms causing heterogeneous detection associated with particular parameters were somewhat unclear. For example, age-0 suckers were more likely to be detected in cooler water or offshore, and age-1 suckers were more likely to be detected nearshore or in environments with larger substrates. These results may indicate more movement or higher densities of suckers under these conditions. Regardless of the cause, modeling heterogeneity in detection allowed us to generate unbiased estimates of occupancy.

Summary

Age-0 suckers in Upper Klamath Lake are primarily habitat generalists, whereas age-1 suckers are found less frequently and use environments with characteristics similar to environments used by adult suckers. Age-0 sucker presence is best predicted by water temperatures common during July and August and by water depths found commonly throughout Upper Klamath Lake (2–3 m). This result is corroborated by previous occupancy models on age-0 suckers that reported only slight trends in age-0 sucker habitat use with respect to environmental variables . Age-1 suckers have a slight tendency to select in-lake environments with water depths of 4–5 m, with large substrate such as boulder, and may be moving between nearshore and offshore areas throughout the summer. All these observed patterns are inconclusive, however, given that they are drawn from weak trends in data collected in a single year. All analyses were conducted on suckers as a whole. Some of the uncertainty in our results may be due to differential habitat use among sucker species. Therefore, future research should focus on differentiating habitat use by sucker species and clarifying the trends in age-1 sucker habitat use.

References Cited

Bailey, L.L., Simons, T.R., and Pollock, K.H., 2004, Spatial and temporal variation in detection probability of plethodon salamanders using the robust capture-recapture design: Journal of Wildlife Management, v. 68, p. 14-24.

Bayley, P.B., and Peterson, J.T., 2001, An approach to estimating the probability of presence and richness of fish species: Transactions of the American Fisheries Society, v. 130, no. 4, p. 620-633.

Banish, N.P., Adams, B.J., and Shivley, R.S., 2009, Distribution and habitat associations of radio-tagged adult Lost River sucker and shortnose sucker in Upper Klamath Lake, Oregon: Transactions of the American Fisheries Society, v. 138, no. 1, p. 153-168.

Beyer, H.L., 2006, Hawth's Analysis Tools for ArcGIS: Accessed February 25, 2009, at http://www.spatialecology.com/htools.

Buettner, M., and Scoppettone, G.G., 1990, Life history and status of Catostomids in Upper Klamath Lake, Oregon: Seattle, Wash., U.S. Fish and Wildlife Service, National Fisheries Research Center, contract completion report, 108 p.

Burdick, S.M, Wilkens, A.X., and VanderKooi, S.P., 2008a, Nearshore and offshore habitat use by endangered juvenile Lost River and shortnose suckers in Upper Klamath Lake, Oregon: U.S. Geological Survey Open-File Report 2007-1356, 30 p.

Burdick, S.M., Hendrixson, H.A., and VanderKooi, S.P., 2008b, Age-0 Lost River and shortnose sucker nearshore habitat use in Upper Klamath Lake, Oregon: A patch-occupancy approach: Transactions of the American Fisheries Society, v. 137, p. 417-430.

Burnham, K.P., and Anderson, D.R., 2002, Model selection and multimodel inference: a practical information-theoretic approach (2nd ed.): New York, Springer, 496 p.

Cooch, E., and White, G., 2008, Program MARK: a gentle introduction (7th ed): Fort Collins, Colo., Colorado State University, accessed February 17, 2009, at http://www.phidot.org/software/mark/docs/book/.

Eliers, J.M., and Eliers, B.J., 2007, Fish habitat analysis of Upper Klamath Lake and Agency Lake, Oregon – completion report to Bureau of Reclamation, Klamath Falls, Oregon: Bend, Oreg., J.C. Headwaters, Inc., 37 p.

Guy, C.S., and Brown, M.L., 2007, Analysis and interpretation of freshwater fisheries data: Bethesda, Md., American Fisheries Society, 961 p.

Beyer, H.L., 2006, Hawth's Analysis Tools for ArcGIS: Accessed February 27, 2009, at http://www.spatialecology.com/htools.

Hendrixson, H.A., Burdick, S.M., Herring, B.L., and VanderKooi, S.P., 2007a, Nearshore and offshore habitat use by endangered, juvenile Lost River and shortnose suckers in Upper Klamath Lake, Oregon: Annual Report 2004: U.S. Geological Survey, Western Fisheries Research Center, Klamath Falls Field Station, 57 p.

Hendrixson, H.A., Burdick, S.M., Wilkens, A.X., and VanderKooi, S.P., 2007b, Nearshore and offshore habitat use by endangered, juvenile Lost River and shortnose suckers in Upper Klamath Lake, Oregon: Annual Report 2005: U.S. Geological Survey, Western Fisheries Research Center, Klamath Falls Field Station.

Loftus, M.E., 2001, Assessment of potential water quality stress to fish, Supplement to effects of water quality and lake level on the biology and habitat of selected fish species in Upper Klamath Lake: Redmond, Wash., R2 Resource Consultants, Inc., report prepared for the Bureau of Indian Affairs, Portland, Oreg.

MacKenzie, D.L., 2005, Was it there? Dealing with imperfect detection for species presence/absence data: Australian and New Zealand Journal of Statistics, v. 47, p. 65-74.

MacKenzie, D.L., Nichols, J.D., Royle, J.A., Pollock, K.H., Bailey, L.L., and Hines, J.E., 2006, Occupancy estimation and modeling: inferring patterns and dynamics of species occurrence: San Francisco, Calif., Elsevier Publishing, 344 p.

Markle, D.F., Cavalluzzi, M.R., and Simon, D.C., 2005, Morphology and taxonomy of Klamath Basin suckers (Catostomidae): Western North American Naturalist, v. 65, no. 4, p. 473-489.

Markle, D.F., and Clauson, K., 2006, Ontogenetic and spatial changes in diet of late larval and juvenile suckers (Catostomidae) in Upper Klamath Lake, Oregon: Western North American Naturalist, v. 66, no. 4, p. 492-501.

Martin, B.A., and Saiki, M.K., 1999, Effects of ambient water quality on the endangered Lost River sucker in Upper Klamath Lake, Oregon: Transactions of the American Fisheries Society, v. 128, p. 953-961.

National Research Council, 2004, Endangered and threatened fishes in the Klamath River Basin: Washington, D.C., The National Academies Press, 397 p.

Peterson, J.T., Thurow, R.T., and Guzevich, J.W., 2004, An evaluation of multipass electrofishing for estimating the abundance of stream dwelling salmonids: Transactions of the American Fisheries Society, v. 133, p. 462-475.

Saiki, M.K., Monda, D.P., and Bellurud, B.L., 1999, Lethal levels of selected water quality variables to larval and juvenile Lost River and shortnose suckers: Environmental Pollution, v. 105, p. 37-44.

Terwilliger, M.R., Simon, D.C., and Markle, D.F., 2004, Larval and juvenile ecology of Upper Klamath Lake suckers, 1995–2003: Corvallis, Oreg., Oregon Cooperative Research Unit, Department of Fisheries and Wildlife, Oregon State University.

VanderKooi, S.P., and Buelow, K.A., 2003, Nearshore habitat use by endangered juvenile suckers in Upper Klamath Lake, Oregon: Annual Report 2001: U.S. Geological Survey, Western Fisheries Research Center, Klamath Falls Field Station.

VanderKooi, S.P., Hendrixson, H.A., Herring, B.L., and Coshow, R.H., 2007, Nearshore habitat use by endangered juvenile suckers in Upper Klamath Lake, Oregon: Annual Report 2002–2003: U.S. Geological Survey, Western Fisheries Research Center, Klamath Falls Field Station.

Weir, L.A., Royle, J.A., Nanjappa, P., and Jung, R.E., 2005, Modeling anuran detection and site occupancy on North American amphibian monitoring program (NAAMP) routes in Maryland: Journal of Herpetology, v. 39, p. 627-639.

Wood, T. M., Hoilman, G.R., and Lindenberg, M.K., 2006, Water quality conditions in Upper Klamath Lake, Oregon, 2002–2004. U.S. Geological Survey Scientific Investigations Report 2006-5209, 52 p.

White, G.C., and Burnham, K.P., 1999, Program MARK: Survival estimation from populations of marked animals: Bird Study, v. 46, supplement, p. 120-138.

Table 1. List of variables used in habitat use and detection probability logit submodels.

[Biological inferences of each variable to either habitat use or detection probability are given. Abbreviations given are used in AIC tables (tables 3 and 4) for simplification]

Predictor variable	Abbreviation	Biological inference to habitat use (occupancy)	Biological inference to detection probability
Presence of predators	PREDPRES	The portion of used habitat use varies with the presence or absence of predators (yellow perch, pumpkinseed, brown bullhead, or rainbow trout over 100 mm SL). Only modeled for age-0 suckers.	-
Species richness	SRTOTAL	The portion of habitat used varies with the total number of non-sucker species present.	-
Substrate (in two classes small and large)	SUBSTRATE	The portion of habitat used varies by substrate (in two classes small and large)	Density of suckers varies by substrate size, and therefore affects detection probability
Depth	DEPTH	The portion of habitat used varies with depth. A polynomial was used so that habitat use may be maximized at some intermediate depth.	Detection probability is influenced by depth.
Area	AREA	The portion of habitat used varies by area (north, central, or south)	-
Soak Time	SOAKTIME	-	Detection probability is influenced by the number of hours a net is fished
Distance from shore	NEAR-OFF	The portion of habitat used is different in nearshore areas than offshore areas.	Swimming behavior or density are different in nearshore areas than offshore areas and cause differential detection between the two
Temperature averaged over the 6 days prior to sampling and the day of sampling.	7DAYMEANT	The portion of habitat used varies with mean temperature calculated for the week proceeding sampling	-
Temperature averaged over the duration of the net set	NETSETTEMP	-	Mean daily temperature affects the behavior of juvenile suckers and therefore influences detection probability
pH averaged over the 6 days prior to sampling and the day of sampling.	7DAYMEANPH	The portion of habitat used varies with mean pH calculated for the week proceeding sampling	-
pH averaged over the 6 days prior to sampling and the day of sampling and scaled to a value between 0 and 1 based on Loftus and others (2001) stress index	PHSI	The portion of habitat used varies by the amount of stress induced by pH	-
Dissolved oxygen concentration averaged over the 6 days prior to sampling and the day of sampling.	7DAYMEANDO	The portion of habitat used varies with mean dissolved oxygen calculated for the week proceeding sampling	-
Dissolved oxygen concentration averaged over the 6 days prior to sampling and the day of sampling and scaled to a value between 0 and 1 based on Loftus and others (2001) stress index	DOSI	The portion of habitat used varies by the amount of stress induced by low DO	-
Month	MONTH	The portion of used habitats varies by month from June to September	-
Month by area interaction	MONTH*AREA	The portion of habitat used varies by a month by area interaction. This may occur if there was a directed migration from one area to another between June and September	-
Month by depth interaction	MONTH*DEPTH	The portion of habitat used at different depths varies among months	-
Month by distance from shore	MONTH*NEAR-OFF	The portion of habitat used in near or offshore strata varies among months	-

Table 2. Occupancy models fit to age-0 sucker presence-absence data.

[The letter p proceeds detection probability parameters and ψ proceeds habitat use parameters used in logit submodels. A dot (.) indicates no submodel parameters were used. The null model (0-23) has no submodel parameters for either detection or habitat use. The goodness of fit was tested for the global model (0-40), which has the most parameters. The biological inferences made from each model parameter are given in table 1. Akaike Information Criteria with a small sample size adjustment (AICc) and AICc weights are given. AICc weights indicate the probability that a model is the best one in the set of models. Confidence models highlighted with bold text indicate the most important parameters for estimating habitat use and detection probability]

Model	AICc Weights	Model Number	AICc	Num. Par
p(NETSETTEMP) ψ (7DAYMEANT+7DAYMEANT^2)	**0.647**	**0-1**	**665.44**	**5**
p(.) ψ (7DAYMEANT+7DAYMEANT^2)	**0.353**	**0-2**	**666.66**	**4**
p(.) ψ (PREDPRES)	9.590E-18	0-3	742.95	3
p(.) ψ (SRTOTAL)	5.329E-18	0-4	744.12	3
p(.) ψ ((DEPTH+DEPTH^2)+MONTH)	3.167E-20	0-5	754.37	8
p(.) ψ (DEPTH+ DEPTH^2)	1.878E-20	0-6	755.42	4
p(DEPTH) ψ ((DEPTH+DEPTH^2)+MONTH)	1.148E-20	0-7	756.40	9
p(DEPTH) ψ (DEPTH+DEPTH^2)	6.964E-21	0-8	757.40	5
p(MONTH) ψ ((DEPTH+DEPTH^2)+MONTH)	1.403E-21	0-9	760.61	11
p(MONTH) ψ ((DEPTH+DEPTH^2)+MONTH + (DEPTH+DEPTH^2)*MONTH)	1.342E-21	0-10	760.70	15
p(.) ψ (PHSI)	1.198E-21	0-11	760.92	3
p(.) ψ ((DEPTH+DEPTH^2)+MONTH + (DEPTH+DEPTH^2)*MONTH)	4.231E-22	0-12	763.00	16
p(.) ψ (MONTH)	2.220E-22	0-13	764.29	5
p(DEPTH) ψ ((DEPTH+DEPTH^2)+MONTH + (DEPTH+DEPTH^2)*MONTH)	1.463E-22	0-14	765.13	17
p(.) ψ (MONTH + NEAR-OFF)	1.328E-22	0-15	765.32	7
p(.) ψ (7DAYMEANDO)	1.282E-22	0-16	765.39	3
p(NEAR-OFF) ψ (MONTH + NEAR-OFF)	1.249E-22	0-17	765.45	8
p(.) ψ (DOSI)	7.442E-23	0-18	766.48	3
p(NEAR-OFF) ψ (.)	5.743E-23	0-19	767.00	3
p(NEAR-OFF) ψ (NEAR-OFF)	4.799E-23	0-20	767.36	4
p(NETSETTEMP) ψ (.)	4.690E-23	0-21	767.40	3
p(.) ψ (NEAR-OFF)	4.681E-23	0-22	767.41	3
p(.) ψ (.)	2.970E-23	0-23	768.32	2
p(DEPTH) ψ (.)	2.604E-23	0-24	768.58	3
p(.) ψ (MONTH + AREA)	2.105E-23	0-25	769.01	8
p(SUBSTRATE) ψ (.)	1.916E-23	0-26	769.19	3
p(.) ψ (SUBSTRATE)	1.236E-23	0-27	770.07	3
p(SOAKTIME) ψ (.)	1.230E-23	0-28	770.08	3
p(.) ψ (7DAYMEANPH)	1.092E-23	0-29	770.32	3
p(MONTH) ψ (MONTH)	1.036E-23	0-30	770.42	8
p(.) ψ (AREA)	7.455E-24	0-31	771.08	4
p(SUBSTRATE) ψ (SUBSTRATE)	7.102E-24	0-32	771.18	4
p(MONTH) ψ (MONTH +NEAR-OFF)	5.972E-24	0-33	771.53	10
p(MONTH) ψ (.)	2.979E-24	0-34	772.92	5
p(.) ψ (NEAR-OFF + MONTH + MONTH*NEAR-OFF)	2.255E-24	0-35	773.47	15
p(NEAR-OFF) ψ (NEAR-OFF + MONTH + MONTH*NEAR-OFF)	2.126E-24	0-36	773.59	16
p(MONTH) ψ (MONTH +AREA) }	1.085E-25	0-37	779.54	13
p(MONTH) ψ (NEAR-OFF + MONTH + MONTH*NEAR-OFF)	8.705E-26	0-38	779.98	18
p(.) ψ (MONTH + AREA + MONTH*AREA)	7.821E-28	0-39	789.41	20
p(MONTH) ψ (MONTH+AREA+MONTH*AREA)	2.712E-30	0-40	800.74	25

Table 3. Occupancy models fit to age-1 sucker presence-absence data. The letter p proceeds detection probability parameters and ψ proceeds habitat use parameters used in logit submodels.

[A dot (.) indicates no submodel parameters were used. The null model (1-27) has not submodel parameters for either detection or habitat use. The goodness of fit was tested for the global model (1-39), which has the most parameters. The biological inferences made from each model parameter are given in table 1. Variance inflated Akaike Information Criteria with a small sample size adjustment (QAICc) and QAICc weights are given. QAICc weights are the probability that a model is the best one in the set of models. Confidence models highlighted with bold text contain the most important parameters for estimating habitat use and detection probability]

Model	QAICc Weights	Model Number	QAICc	Number of Parameters
p(NEAR-OFF) ψ (MONTH + NEAR-OFF)	**0.157**	**1-1**	**614.4743**	**8**
p(DEPTH) ψ (DEPTH+DEPTH^2+MONTH)	**0.131**	**1-2**	**614.8284**	**8**
p(DEPTH) ψ (DEPTH+DEPTH^2+MONTH + (DEPTH+DEPTH^2)MONTH)	**0.111**	**1-3**	**615.1616**	**17**
p(.) ψ (DEPTH+DEPTH^2+MONTH)	**0.093**	**1-4**	**615.5151**	**8**
p(SUBSTRATE) ψ (.)	**0.074**	**1-5**	**615.9804**	**3**
p(SUBSTRATE) ψ (SUBSTRATE)	**0.070**	**1-6**	**616.0905**	**4**
p(.) ψ (SUBSTRATE)	**0.056**	**1-7**	**616.5237**	**3**
p(.) ψ (DEPTH+DEPTH^2)	**0.054**	**1-8**	**616.6005**	**4**
p(DEPTH) ψ (DEPTH+DEPTH^2)	**0.034**	**1-9**	**617.5243**	**5**
p(.) ψ (DEPTH+DEPTH^2+MONTH + (DEPTH+DEPTH^2)MONTH)	**0.032**	**1-10**	**617.6434**	**16**
p(NEAR-OFF) ψ (.)	**0.026**	**1-11**	**618.0929**	**3**
p(.) ψ (MONTH + NEAR-OFF)	0.015	1-12	619.1393	7
p(MONTH) ψ (DEPTH+DEPTH^2+MONTH)	0.015	1-13	619.1412	11
p(.) ψ (MONTH)	0.014	1-14	619.3447	5
p(NEAR-OFF) ψ (NEAR-OFF)	0.009	1-15	620.1343	4
p(MONTH) ψ (DEPTH+DEPTH^2+MONTH + (DEPTH+DEPTH^2)+MONTH)	0.008	1-16	620.3051	19
p(MONTH) ψ (.)	0.005	1-17	621.3421	5
p(.) ψ (7DAYMEANT+7DAYMEANT^2)	0.005	1-18	621.4804	4
p(.) ψ (7DAYDOSI)	0.004	1-19	622.0664	3
p(.) ψ (NEAR-OFF)	0.003	1-20	622.1902	3
p(SOAKTIME) ψ (.)	0.003	1-21	622.7265	3
p(.) ψ (MONTH+AREA)	0.002	1-22	622.9218	8
p(MONTH) ψ (MONTH +NEAR-OFF)	0.002	1-23	623.1704	10
p(NETSETTEMP) ψ (7DAYMEANT+7DAYMEANT^2)	0.002	1-24	623.2043	5
p(.) ψ (7DAYMEANDO)	0.001	1-25	623.8044	3
p(MONTH) ψ (MONTH)	0.001	1-26	624.041	8
p(.) ψ (.)	6.145E-04	1-27	625.5542	2
p(.) ψ (AREA)	4.491E-04	1-28	626.1814	4
p(.) ψ (7DAYMEANPH)	4.344E-04	1-29	626.2479	3
p(DEPTH) ψ (.)	3.226E-04	1-30	626.8434	3
p(NETSETTEMP) ψ (.)	2.747E-04	1-31	627.1646	3
p(.) ψ (SRTOTAL)	2.642E-04	1-32	627.2429	3
p(.) ψ (7DAYPHSI)	2.477E-04	1-33	627.3714	3
p(NEAR-OFF) ψ (MONTH + NEAR-OFF+ MONTH*NEAR-OFF)	1.510E-04	1-34	628.3615	16
p(.) ψ (MONTH + NEAR-OFF+ MONTH*NEAR-OFF)	5.878E-05	1-35	630.2482	15
p(MONTH) ψ (MONTH + AREA)	3.222E-05	1-36	631.4507	13
p(MONTH) ψ (MONTH + NEAR-OFF+ MONTH*NEAR-OFF)	4.632E-06	1-37	635.3299	18
p(.) ψ (MONTH + AREA + MONTH*AREA)	2.133E-08	1-38	646.0908	20
p(MONTH) ψ (MONTH + AREA + MONTH*AREA)	1.524E-10	1-39	655.9745	25

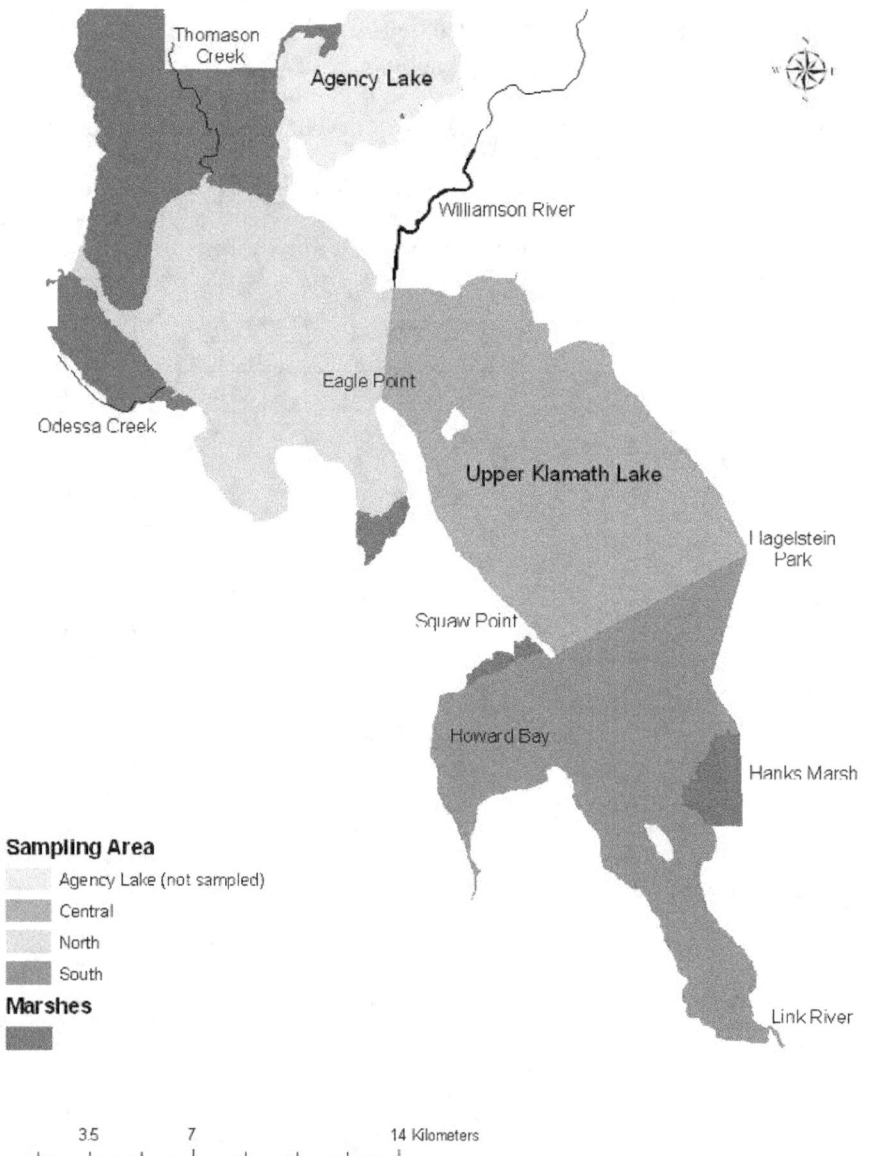

Figure 1. Map of areas in Upper Klamath Lake sampled for juvenile suckers in 2007. Sampling was stratified to include nearshore (≤ 100 m) and offshore (> 100 m) strata in three areas of the lake. We defined the three areas as: north and west of Eagle Point and the mouth of the Williamson River (North), south and east of Eagle Point and the mouth of the Williamson River and north of Squaw Point and Hagelstein Park (Central), and south of Hagelstein Park and Squaw Point including Howard Bay (South). An equal number of randomly selected sites were sampled in each stratum.

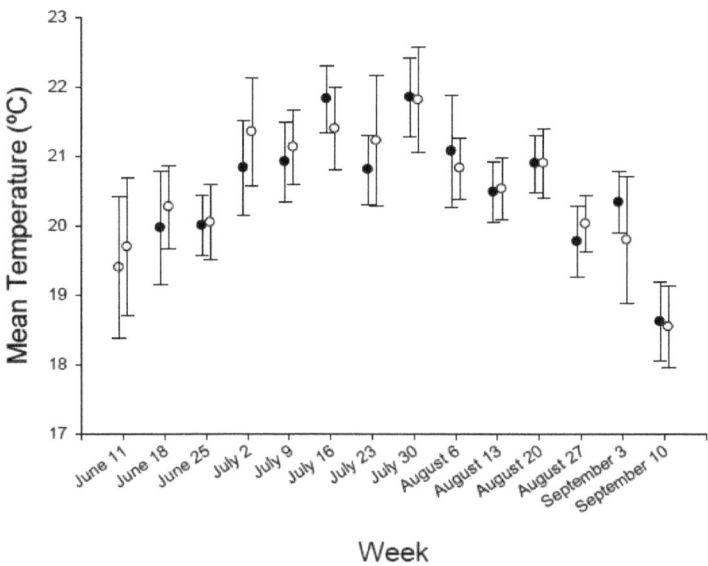

Figure 2. Mean of water temperature means used in models by week. Solid circles represent the 7-day mean temperatures calculated for the six days proceeding sampling and the day of sampling. The open circles represent the mean temperature calculated for the duration of a net set. Standard errors bars are given.

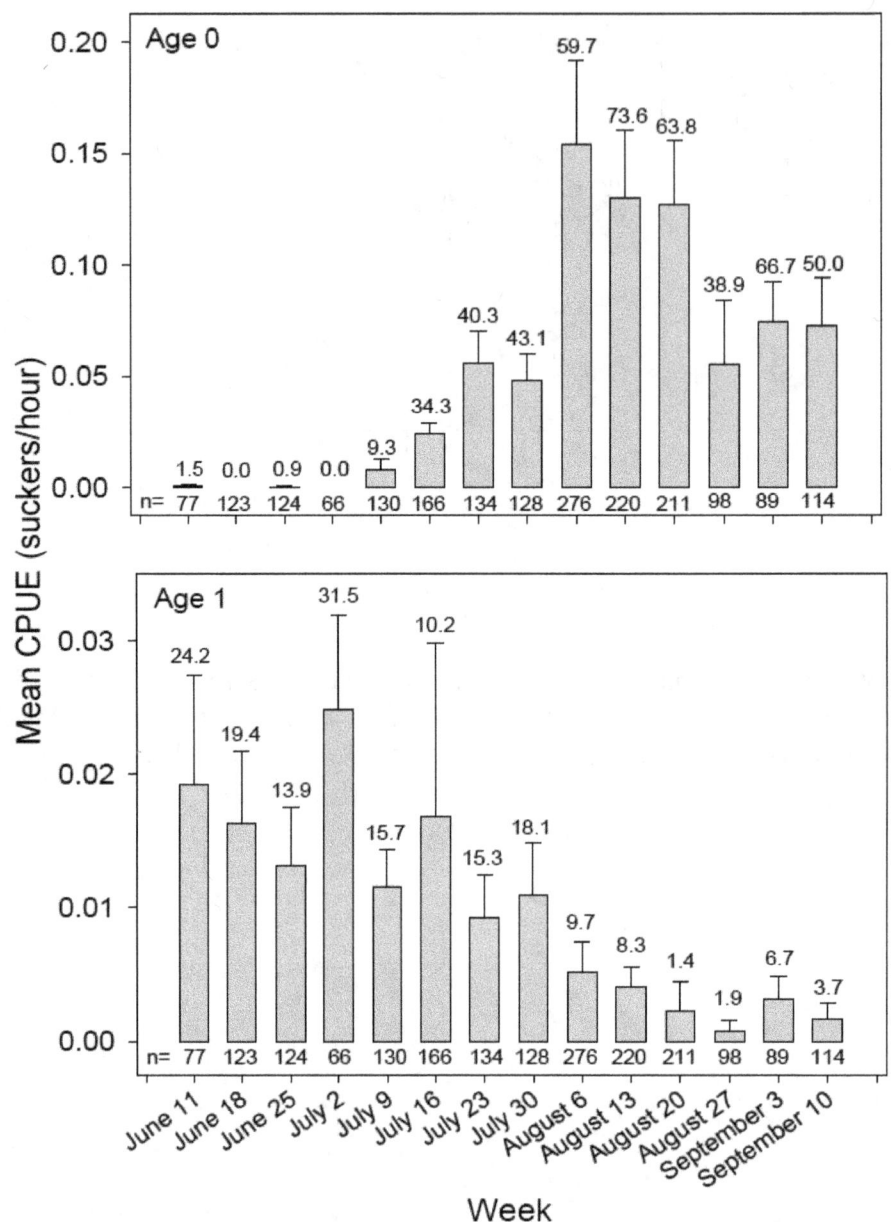

Figure 3. Mean catch per unit effort (CPUE; suckers/hour) ± SE by age and week for juvenile Lost River and shortnose suckers captured in Upper Klamath Lake, Oregon, from early June to mid-September 2007. The number of samples collected each week (n) and the percentage of nets to catch at least one sucker also are given. The scale of the y-axis is different in the two graphs.

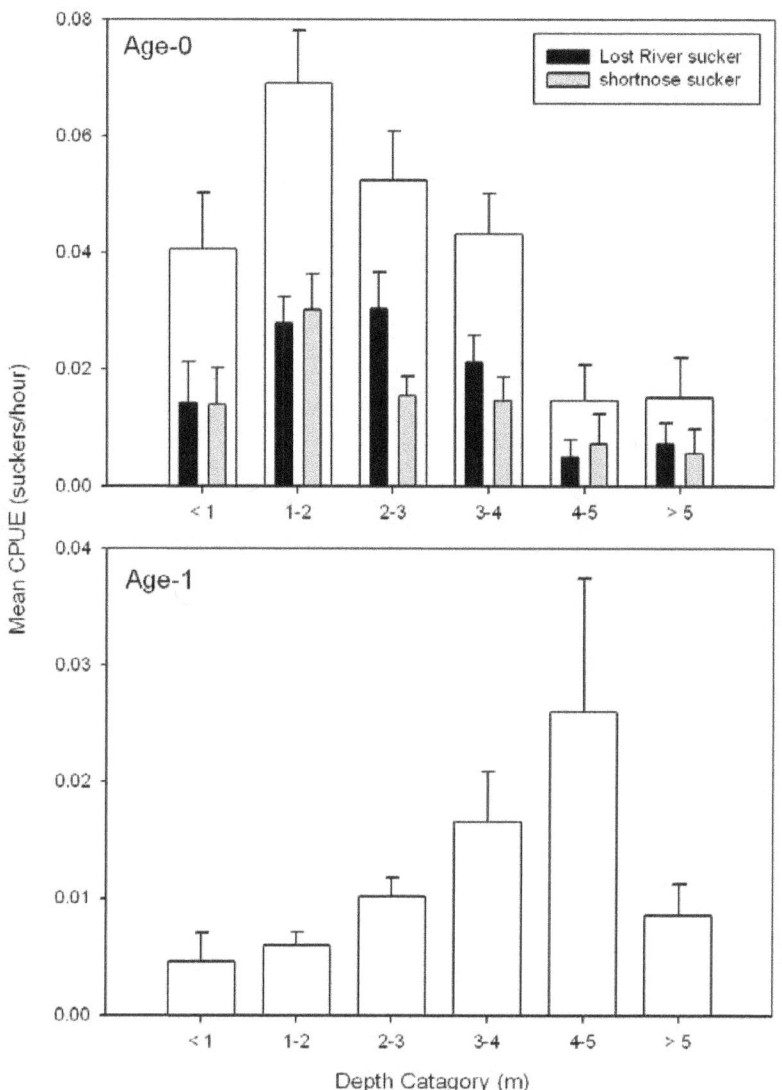

Figure 4. Mean catch per unit effort (CPUE; sucker/hour) + SE for age-0 and age-1 suckers by water depth (m), in Upper Klamath Lake, Oregon, caught from early June to mid-September 2007. CPUE for both species combined (white bars) is given for both age-0 and age-1 suckers. The scale of the y-axis is different in the two graphs. CPUE was estimated for age-0 fish of each species using data from a subsample of sacrificed suckers (about 30 percent) and extrapolating to the entire catch. A similar extrapolation was not done for age-1 suckers because the subsample was too small to be representative.

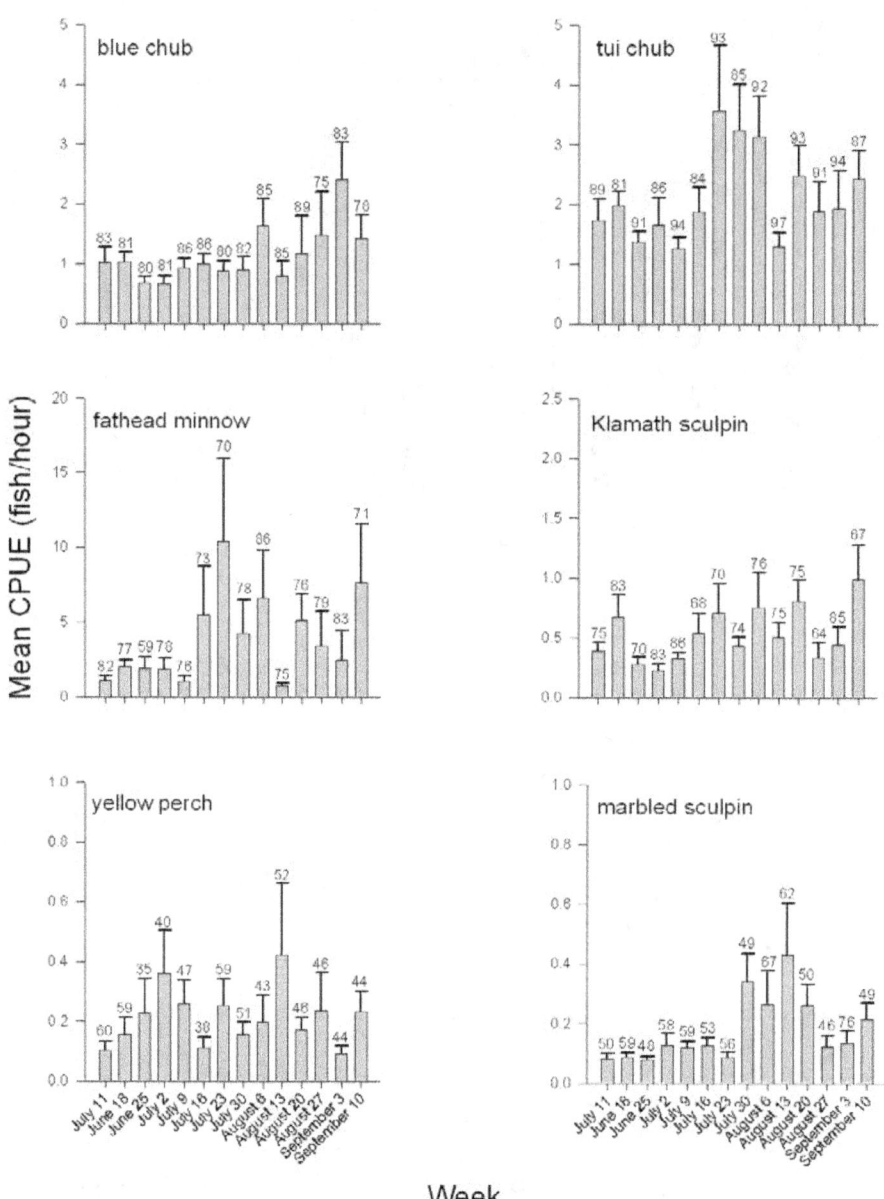

Figure 5. Mean catch per unit effort (CPUE) and standard error for the six most common species in Upper Klamath Lake, Oregon, by week in 2007. The percentages of nets that caught at least one of each species each week are also given. Note that the scale of the *y*-axis is different among graphs.

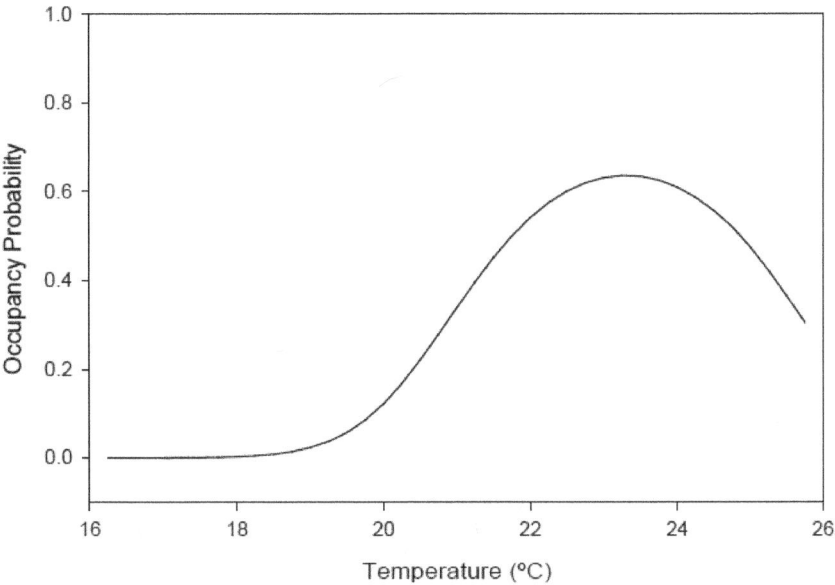

Figure 6. Probability that a site was used by an age-0 sucker given water temperature (°C) calculated for the 6 days proceeding sampling and the day of sampling. In-lake environments with a mean temperature of 23.3 °C had the highest probability of occupancy (0.66). Confidence intervals encompassed both 0 and 1 at all temperatures, suggesting this result should be interpreted as insignificant.

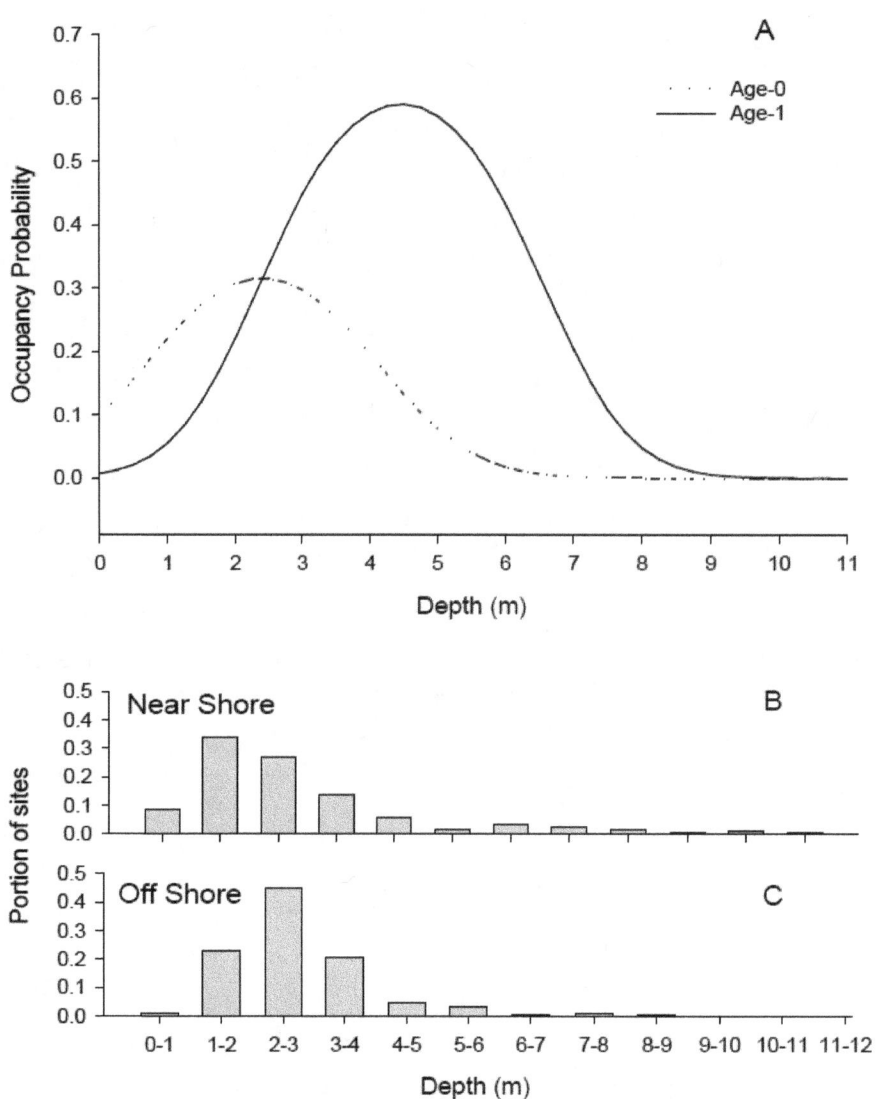

Figure 7. Probability of site occupancy by age-0 and age-1 suckers by (*A*) water depth, (*B*) proportion of total sites at each depth sampled nearshore, and (*C*) offshore. Because sample sites were chosen using stratified random design, sampled depths represent available depths in both nearshore and offshore environments. There was no statistical difference in median depths sampled in nearshore and offshore sites (Mann-Whitney U test $p = 0.03$). Habitat use was maximized at 2.4 m deep for age-0 suckers and 4.4 m deep for age-1 suckers. Confidence bands for selection curves encompassed both 0 and 1 at the entire range of depths sampled.

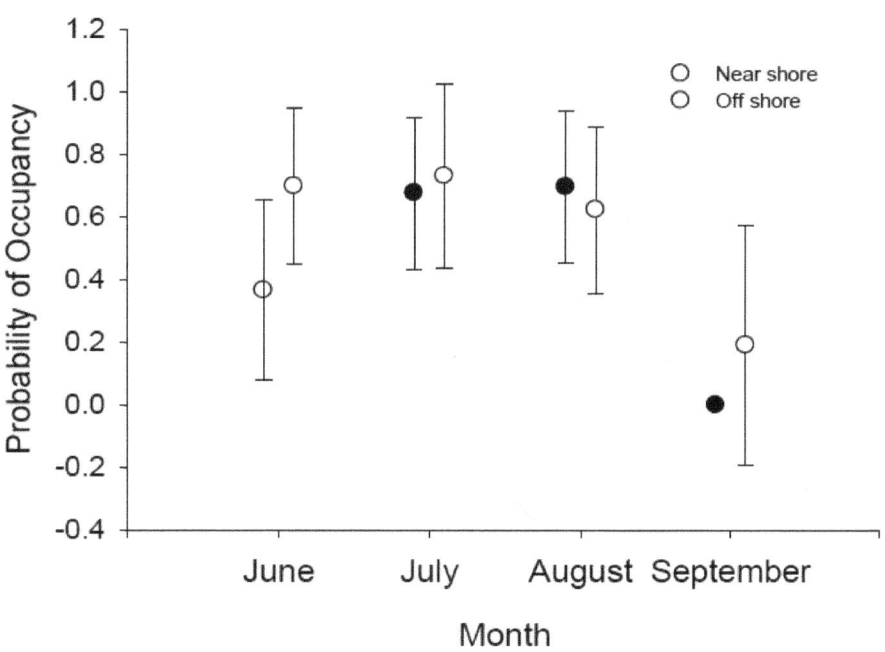

Figure 8. Probability of age-0 sucker occupancy ± 1 SE in nearshore and offshore areas of Upper Klamath Lake, Oregon, during 2007 by month. Nearshore sites were within 100 m of shore, whereas offshore sites were more than 100 m from shore.

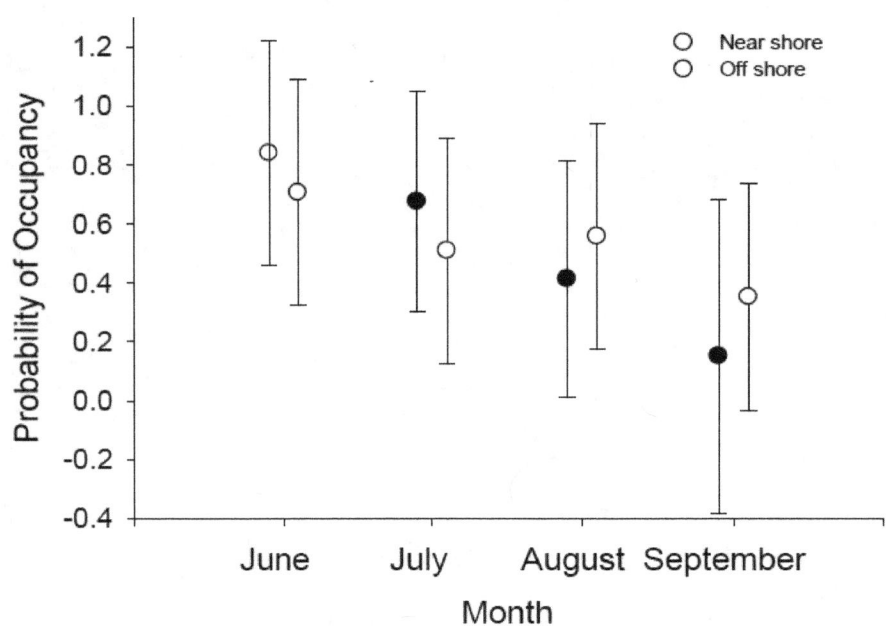

Figure 9. Probability of age-1 sucker occupancy ± 1 SE in nearshore and offshore areas of Upper Klamath Lake, Oregon, in 2007 by month. Nearshore sites were within 100 m of shore, whereas offshore sites were more than 100 m from shore.

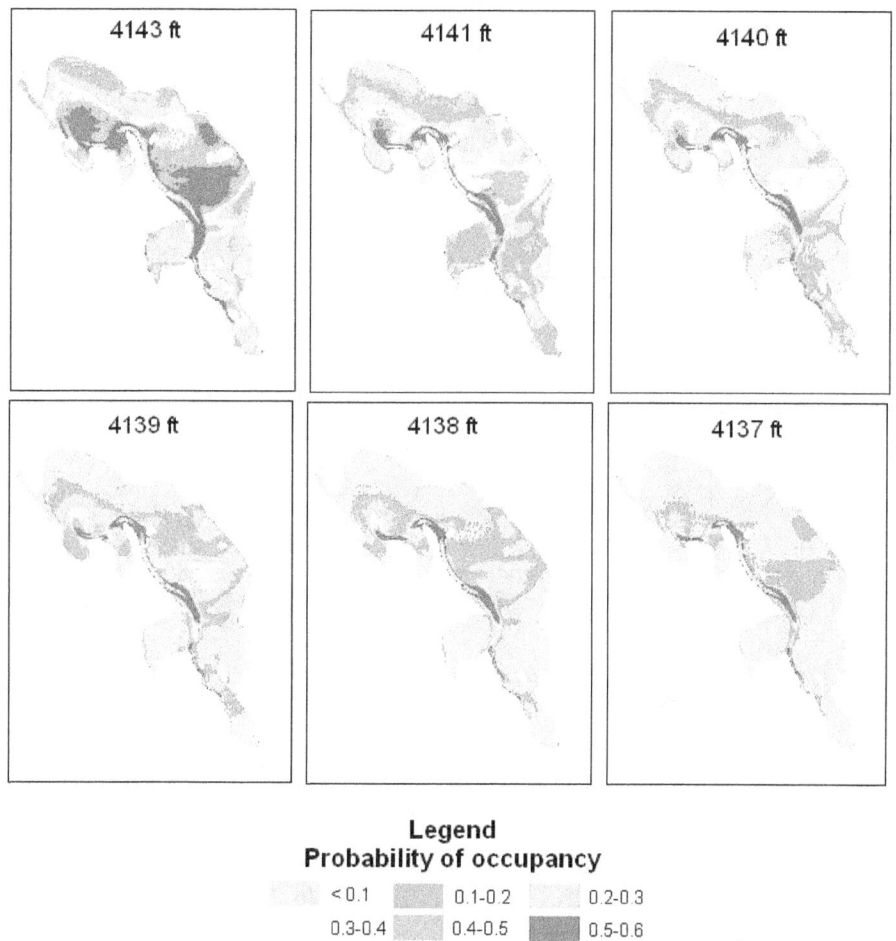

Figure 10. Probability of age-1 sucker site occupancy based on depth throughout Upper Klamath Lake, Oregon, in 2007 at six lake levels: near full pool 4,143 ft (1,262.8 m); 4,141 ft (1,262.2); 4,140 ft (1,262.0); 4,139 ft (1,261.6 m); 4,138 ft (1,261.3), and the new proposed minimum lake level of 4,137 ft (1,260.9 m).

Chapter 3.—Tag Loss and the Effects of Passive Integrated Transponder (PIT) Tagging on Mortality of Age-1 Lost River Suckers

By Summer M. Burdick, U.S. Geological Survey

Introduction

Despite extensive research on Lost River sucker *Deltistes luxatus* and shortnose sucker *Chasmistes brevirostris* in Upper Klamath Lake, Oregon, relatively little information exists on juvenile survival, movement, growth rates, and age to maturity. Because of rapidly declining catch rates over time, juvenile Lost River and shortnose sucker survival rates are thought to be extremely low (VanderKooi and Buelow, 2003; Hendrixson and others, 2007; VanderKooi and others, 2007; Simon and Markle, 2008). Traditional methods (for example, catch curves and cohort analysis) of estimating survival, however, depend on the critical yet difficult to meet assumptions of constant catchability among age classes and gear types. Migration of age-0 suckers from north to south along the eastern shore of Upper Klamath Lake has been inferred by comparing temporal and spatial trends in catch rates along the eastern shore of Upper Klamath Lake (Gutermuth and others, 2000; Simon and Markle, 2006; Hendrixson and others, 2007; VanderKooi and others, 2007). Age to maturity and growth rates of Lost River and shortnose suckers were estimated from otoliths and opercula (Buettner and Scoppettone, 1990; B.J. Adams, U.S. Geological Survey, written commun., 2006). Ages, however, have not been validated for either species. Given that annuli in calcified structures form at different rates depending on species, validation of aging techniques for each species is critical (Beamish and McFarlane, 1983).

Tagging studies offer a quantitative way to estimate survival rates, migration rates and patterns, age to maturity, and growth rates. For example, survival can be estimated while accounting for differences in detection probabilities among age classes and gear types using mark-recapture techniques. Marking fish can refine our understanding of migration patterns and allow direct estimates of movement rates. Mark-recapture techniques also allow growth rates and age to maturity to be measured directly.

For a tag to be useful in mark-recapture studies, it should not alter survival and should have a high retention rate (Pine and others, 2003). This is because mark-recapture (for example, Cormack-Jolly-Seber) and tag recovery (for example, Brownie models) techniques rely on the assumptions that the population of tagged individuals has a similar mortality rate as the population as a whole and that tags are not lost or overlooked (Williams and others, 2002). Tagging induced mortality and tag loss can cause a negative bias in survival estimates if unaccounted for (Brownie and others, 1985; Pine and others, 2003), thus making accurate estimates of these rates difficult.

Few tagging methods exist that allow small fish to be uniquely marked, which is a requirement of all but the most rudimentary mark-recapture models (Pine and others, 2003). Small fish tend to have higher rates of tagging induced mortality and lower rates of recapture than larger fish, thus creating unique challenges for biologists. One option that meets tagging requirements is the passive integrated transponder (PIT) tag. These tags have unique identification numbers, high retention rates, infinite life, and are relatively inexpensive. In addition, PIT tags can be read remotely, increasing the number of recapture tag encounters while reducing handling stress (Zydlewski and others, 2006).

Passive integrated transponder tag loss rates (Gries and Letcher, 2002) and the effects of PIT tagging on survival (Prentice and others, 1990; Ombredane and others, 1998; Gries and Letcher, 2002; Bateman and Gresswell, 2006) and growth (Prentice and others, 1990; Ombredane and others, 1998; Bateman and Gresswell, 2006) have been extensively studied for juvenile salmonids *Oncorhynchus* spp. Tag induced mortality and tag retention rates, however, likely vary among species. Similar published estimates of survival and tag loss for catostomids are limited to a single study of bluehead chub *Catostomus discobolus* (164 to 278 mm total length; Ward and David, 2006), despite the fact that catostomids of similar or smaller or size are routinely given PIT tags in studies designed to examine movement or survival (Douglas and Marsh, 1998; Ward and David, 2006). Ward and others (2008) determined gut fullness to be a significant factor in post PIT-tagging survival for two species of endangered *Gila*. In this chapter, we describe the results of our investigation of tag-loss rates and effects of surgical implantation of the survival of juvenile suckers. These results should help to determine the usefulness of PIT tags for future studies of juvenile Lost River and shortnose suckers.

Methods

We used a two-phased approach to examine short-term PIT tag loss and the effects of PIT tagging on juvenile sucker survival. We began by implanting tags in first generation hatchery-reared Lost River suckers, which were kept in a controlled environment during experimentation. We then tagged wild age-1 Lost River and shortnose suckers caught and held in Upper Klamath Lake. This approach allowed us to assess the effects of PIT tagging on survival in two different environments.

Laboratory Methods

Study fish were offspring of three adult Lost River suckers of each sex collected from springs along the eastern shore of Upper Klamath Lake on April 18, 2006. To fertilize eggs, an equal volume of milt from each male and eggs from each female were collected and pooled for a ratio of about 1 mL of milt for every 1,000 eggs (R. Stone, U.S. Fish and Wildlife Service, written commun., 2008). Adult suckers were released at the same location where they were captured immediately after artificially spawning. Fertilized eggs were transferred to the California-Nevada Fish Health Center in Anderson, California, where they were incubated in monolayers suspended on top of fine netting within multiple 40 L aquaria supplied with 0.2 L/min flow of aerated 12°C water (R. Stone, U.S. Fish and Wildlife Service, written commun., 2008). Larval suckers were feed *Nannochloropsis* algae and rotifers and were reared for 161 days before the tagging experiment began (S. Foott, U.S. Fish and Wildlife Service, written commun., 2008).

We examined the effects of PIT tagging on survival of age-0 suckers following a method described by Bateman and Gresswell (2006), using a completely randomized design and three treatment groups. We randomly assigned one of three treatments to nine tanks, such that there were three tanks for each treatment (tagged, positive control, and control). Juvenile suckers (153) were randomly selected as experiment subjects and divided evenly between tanks (17 suckers/tank). All study fish, regardless of treatment, were transferred to a 0.02 mg/L solution of tricaine methanesulfonate (MS-222) in batches of three. Fish remained in MS-222 solution until they were anesthetized, indicated by cessation of movement. Fish were weighed to the nearest 0.1 g and standard length (SL) was measured to the nearest mm.

An experienced tagger injected one full duplex, 12.45 × 2.02 mm, 0.106 g, 134.2 kHz, cylindrical passive integrated transponder (PIT) tag into the body cavities of each sucker in the tagged group lateral to the midline of the ventral surface posterior to the pectoral fins using a 3.18 cm hypodermic needle. An empty needle of the same dimensions was similarly inserted into the body cavity of fish in the positive control group. Between each injection the needle was sanitized with Nolvasan.

Wounds were not closed with sutures on either positive control or tagged fish. Suckers assigned to the control group were held for 3 to 5 seconds after weighing to simulate handling stress experienced by tagged and positive control fish. All fish were allowed to recover in a bucket of fresh water prior to being transferred to 38 L holding tanks.

Regardless of treatment group, suckers were cared for and handled identically throughout the study. Dissolved oxygen (DO) concentration, pH, and ammonia, were monitored each week day with a Hach Portable LDO HQ20 meter. A hand delivered subsistence ration of 0.046 g of Otohime Weaning feed per fish was administered to each tank during each week day. Tanks were monitored daily for mortalities and all dead fish were removed and examined to determine cause of death. At about 10-day intervals, fish were removed from tanks in batches of five individuals and anesthetized in a solution of 0.02 mg of MS-222 per liter of water. These fish were weighed to the nearest 0.1 g and standard length was measured to the nearest millimeter. Tagged fish were checked for tag retention and tag number was recorded. The weight of the PIT tag was subtracted from weight measurements of tagged fish.

We measured the cross-sectional area and volume of 10 randomly selected suckers from each control tank so that we could estimate the relative size of fish compared to the PIT tags. A thin piece of string was wrapped around each fish at the anterior edge of the dorsal fin three times, which was the widest part of the fish. The length of string was measured and divided by three to calculate circumference (C). The cross-sectional area of each fish was approximated using the equation

$$Area = \frac{C^2}{4\pi}.$$

Volume was measured to the nearest mL by displacing water in a cylindrical measuring flask.

Field Methods

Healthy suckers about 70 mm SL or longer collected during spring sampling (Chapter 1) were injected with PIT tags identical to those used in the laboratory experiment. Suckers that were not emaciated, had no external macroparasites, were free of deformities, and had no lesions or other wounds were considered healthy. Prior to tagging, suckers were anesthetized in a 0.02 to 0.03 mg/L solution of MS-222, which was prepared with lake water. All suckers were allowed to remain in the solution until they did not respond to stimulus (probing with net or stick). The duration of the anesthetic bath, total handling time, and standard length were recorded for each fish. A different tagger than the one participating in the laboratory experiment injected the tags into sucker body cavities using the same protocol as in the laboratory. The tagger in the field experiment was trained but lacked substantial experience with the tag injection method. Between each injection, needles were sterilized with Nolvasan. Wounds were not closed with sutures and no antibiotics were administered.

Tagged suckers were allowed to recover in a bucket of lake water prior to being transferred to 0.21-m³ net pens. No more than 11 suckers were held in a single net pen and one time. Net pens were suspended overnight about 0.5 m off the substrate at the locations where fish were originally captured. Upon retrieval of the pens the number of sucker mortalities and tags lost were recorded, before live suckers were released at their location of capture. Dead suckers were necropsied in the lab to determine if the tag had caused mortality.

Analysis of Data

We calculated the percentage of tag retention for laboratory and field tagged fish separately as 100 multiplied by the number of fish that retained PIT tags divided by the total number of tagged fish surviving to the end of each experiment. Mortality was similarly calculated as 100 times the number of fish that died divided by the total number of fish in each experiment. To examine the effects of total handling time, standard length, and temperature on survival, we summarized data for survivors and non-survivors in each experiment.

Results of Tagging Experiments

Laboratory Experiment

For the laboratory experiment, a total of 51 Lost River suckers were included in each of three groups. At the beginning of the study, Lost River suckers in our laboratory experiment ranged from 61 to 85 mm SL and weighed between 2.9 and 7.5 g. Tag weight (0.106 g) was only 2.30 percent of mean sucker weight. Cross-sectional area of tags was 2.71 percent of the average cross-sectional area of suckers used in our laboratory experiment. Tag volume was only 0.86 percent of average Lost River sucker volume measured on the last day of the laboratory experiment. With these small-tag-to-body size ratios we did not observe any loss of equilibrium in tagged fish.

Overall tag loss and tagging mortality in the laboratory experiment was low. Only one fish expelled its tag, for a total tag loss rate of 2.13 percent. This tag was lost on the last day (day 34) of the experiment. Mortality of control and positive control fish was 0.0 percent when one fish that jumped out of the tank was excluded from analysis. A total of five tagged suckers from two of three treatment tanks died during the experiment, which was equivalent to a mean tagging mortality rate among treatment tanks of 9.8 percent ± 2.0 (mean ± SE). Of the tagged suckers that died during the experiment, four (80 percent) perished within the first two days, and one died during handling on day 21. Tagged fish that died during the laboratory experiment were shorter (66.6 ± 1.7 mm SL) and lighter (3.9 ± 0.3 g) than tagged survivors (71.9 ± 0.7 mm SL; 5.2 ± 0.1 g) on average (mean ±SE). However, there was some overlap in the range of lengths and weights between suckers that died (62 to 71 mm SL; 3.0 to 4.7 g) and those that survived (62 to 84 mm SL; 3.5 to 7.5 g). The percentage of suckers that died during tagging was twice as high for fish less than 70 mm SL (14 percent) than those 70 mm SL or larger (7 percent).

External surgery wounds healed quickly but post-experiment necropsies revealed light to heavy internal bruising on about 40 percent of surviving tagged suckers. Most surgery wounds healed by day 21, and all but one were completely healed by the end of the experiment. Absence of bruising or light bruising appeared to be associated with tags placed closest to the ventral surface. In all four tagged suckers that died shortly after surgery, tags damaged the heart, whereas in survivors tags were several mm posterior to the heart. In the tagged fish that died on day 21 during handling, the tag was in a more posterior position, did not rupture the heart, and no bruising was observed.

Field Experiment

The juvenile suckers used in the field experiment were captured in 13 separate nets on 6 different days between April 23 and May 29 (see Chapter 1). A total of 40 juvenile suckers ranging from 75 to 147 mm SL and averaging 97.2 ± 2.1 mm SL (mean ± SE) were tagged. Overall tagging mortality was higher in the field (17.5 percent) than in the laboratory (9.8 percent) and was directly related to tag placement. Necropsies showed that tag placement in all suckers that died in the field experiment penetrated or displaced the heart. Therefore, despite the fact that all seven mortalities of field tagged suckers occurred on 2 days toward the end of the experiment (May 14 and May 29), when mean (± SE) water temperatures (°C) generally were warmer throughout the lake (May 16, 16.9 ± 0.2 and May 29, 15.5 ± 0.2) than they were at the beginning of the experiment (April 25, 10.5 ± 0.1; Klamath Tribes, unpub. data, 2007), warm temperatures did not appear to be the cause of death. Handling time, measured from when nets were pulled to when fish were released into net pens, ranged from 10 to 82 minutes, and also did not appear to affect survival. Mean handling time was similar between suckers that died (35 ± 4 minutes) and ones that survived (39 ± 10 minutes). Mean length also was similar between survivors (95.5 ± 4.5 mm SL) and non-survivors (97.5 ±2.4 mm SL), and within the field experiment did not appear to be related to survival. Only two suckers, both tagged in Howard Bay on May 29, expelled their tags during overnight retention in net pens, making the overall tag loss rate 5.0 percent.

Tag Loss and the Effects of Tagging on Mortality of Age-1 Lost River Suckers

The 2.1 percent PIT tag loss rate that we measured in the laboratory and the 5.0 percent loss rate measured in the field were similar to what has been reported for age-0 salmonids (0.2 percent to 3.4 percent; Prentice and others, 1990; Ombredane and others, 1998; Gries and Letcher, 2002; Bateman and Gresswell, 2006), but higher than the 0.0 percent tag loss reported for bluehead chub (164-278 mm TL) or *Perca* spp. (Baras and others, 2000; Ward and David, 2006). The duration of both our laboratory and field experiments prohibit us from concluding anything about long-term tag retention rates. Given that a fish expelled a tag 34 days into the laboratory experiment, chronic long-term tag loss is possible, and should be examined in future studies.

External PIT tagging wounds healed within 21 days of surgery in the laboratory and did not appear to interfere with normal activities. Prentice and others (1990) noted even quicker healing time (14 days) in juvenile salmonids for wounds caused by implanting PIT tags using similar methods to ours. We did not observe loss of equilibrium in Lost River suckers due to tagging as has been observed for perch *Perca* spp. when implanted with tags greater than 1.5 percent of their body weight (Baras and others, 2000). For comparison, age-0 steelhead *Oncorhynchus mykiss* were given tags up to 12.5 percent of their body weight without loss of equilibrium (Bateman and Gresswell, 2006).

A PIT tagging effect on mortality, similar to the one we observed for suckers, has not been reported for juvenile salmonids tagged in laboratory settings using similar methods (Prentice and others, 1990; Peterson and others, 1994). However, when PIT tags were inserted through a small incision rather than using a hypodermic needle, mortality rates for juvenile salmonids ranged from 5.7 percent to 21.2 percent (Roussel and others, 2000; Gries and Letcher, 2002; Bateman and Gresswell, 2006) and tagged fish had a higher mortality rate than untagged fish (Bateman and Gresswell, 2006). In our laboratory experiment, the highest sucker mortality rates occurred within 48 hours of tagging. A similar phenomenon was observed by Bateman and Gresswell (2006) who reported mortality for steelhead was highest within 3 days of tagging.

The mortality rate we observed for juvenile suckers tagged in the field (5.0 percent) was similar to the short-term (2 to 6 days) PIT tagging mortality rate (5.5 percent, n=18) observed for 164 to 278 mm total length bluehead chub (Ward and David, 2006). PIT tags implanted by hypodermic needle, however, do not appear to affect survival of juvenile salmonids in the wild (Peterson and others, 1994; Ombredane, 1998). Lost River suckers and blue chub tend to inhabit warmer water than salmonids, however, which is known to favor microbial outbreaks (Baras and others, 2000) and may explain the higher rate of mortality for these species. However, differences in mortality may be related to morphometric or physiological differences among species.

Higher mortality rates in field tagged suckers (17.5 percent) over lab tagged suckers (9.8 percent) were most likely due to tagger skill and tag placement rather than environmental factors experienced by the fish. Tags were located in a more anterior position and punctured or displaced the heart in all but one of the tagged fish that died in either experiment. Taggers in both the laboratory and field experiments were trained prior to each experiment, but the laboratory tagger was more experienced. Conditions experienced in the field such as wind, rocking of the boat, or unlevel operating surfaces may have also contributed to imprecise tag placement. Our findings contrast with those of Bateman and Gresswall (2006), who reported that tagger experience did not explain differences in mortality rates among PIT tagged age-0 steelhead.

Proper tag placement is more likely to be accomplished in larger rather than smaller suckers. In the laboratory, suckers smaller than 70 mm SL appeared to be more vulnerable to tagging mortality than larger fish. However, size did not appear to affect mortality of fish in the field, which were 75 mm SL or larger. Therefore, we recommend limiting use of 12.45 mm PIT tags to Lost River suckers 75 mm SL or greater. Shorter tags (as small as 8 mm) that are now commercially available may allow smaller suckers to be tagged, but their use still needs to be evaluated.

Summary

Results from this study showed that 12.45 mm PIT tags are a viable option for studying movement and mortality rates and estimating age to maturity, for Lost River suckers at least 75 mm SL. Estimates of mortality generated from PIT tagging will, however, need to be adjusted to account for tagging mortality and tag loss rates. Mortality may be reduced if effort is made to improve tagger skill through practice. Because tagging mortality may be variable it should be assessed within any mortality studies on juvenile suckers that use this technology.

Future research should focus on reducing short-term tagging mortality and tag loss, determining the effects of PIT tagging on growth, and determining long-term effects of PIT tagging on survival. New, smaller PIT tags (8.00 mm) should be evaluated to determine if they can reduce tagging mortality, especially on suckers less than 75 mm SL. Long-term effects of tagging on growth and mortality could cause negative bias in growth and mortality estimates for wild populations of PIT tagged suckers, and should be evaluated.

References Cited

Baras, E., Malbrouck, C., Houbart, M., Kestemont, P., and Melard, C., 2000, The effect of PIT tags on growth and physiology of age-0 cultured Perch Perca fluviatilis of variable size: Aquaculture, v. 185, p. 159-173.

Bateman, D.S., and Gresswell, R.E., 2006, Survival and growth of age-0 steelhead after surgical implantation of 23 mm passive integrated transponders: North American Journal of Fisheries Management, v. 26, no. 3, p. 545-550.

Beamish, R.J., and McFarlane, G.A., 1983, The forgotten requirement of age validation in fisheries biology: Transactions of the American Fisheries Society, v. 112, p. 735-743.

Brownie, C., Anderson, D.R., Burnham, K.P., and Robson, D.R., 1985, Statistical inference from band recovery data - A handbook (2nd ed.): U.S. Fish and Wildlife Service, 156 p.

Buettner, M.E., and Scoppettone, G.G., 1990, Life history and status of catastomids in Upper Klamath Lake, Oregon: Seattle, Wash., U.S. Fish and Wildlife Service, National Fisheries Research Center.

Douglas, M.E., and Marsh, P.C., 1998, Population and Survival Estimates of Catostomus latipinnis in Northern Grand Canyon, with Distribution and Abundance of Hybrids with Xyrauchen texanus: Copeia, v. 1998, no. 4, p. 915-925.

Gries, G., and Letcher, B., 2002, Tag retention and survival of Age-0 Atlantic Salmon following surgical implantation with Passive Integrated Transponder tags: North American Journal of Fisheries Management, v. 22, p. 219-222.

Gutermuth, B., Pinkston, E., and Buettner, M., 2000, A-canal fish entrainment 1997 and 1998 with emphasis on endangered suckers: Klamath, Oreg., New Earth/Cell Tech, and Red Bluff, Calif., Natural Resource Scientists, Inc.

Hendrixson, H.A., Burdick, S.M., Herring, B.L., and VanderKooi, S.P., 2007, Nearshore and offshore habitat use by endangered, juvenile Lost River and shortnose suckers in Upper Klamath Lake, Oregon: Annual Report 2005: U.S. Geological Survey, Western Fisheries Research Center, Klamath Falls Field Station.

Ombredane, D., Bagliniere, J.L., and Marchand, F., 1998, The effects of Passive Integrated Transponder tags on survival and growth of juvenile brown trout (Salmo trutta L.) and their use for studying movement in a small river: Hydrobiologia, v. 371-372, p. 99-106.

Peterson, N.P., Prentice, E.F., and Quinn, T.P., 1994, Comparison of Sequential Coded Wire and Passive Integrated Transponder Tags for Assessing Overwinter Growth and Survival of Juvenile Coho Salmon: North American Journal of Fisheries Management, v. 14, p. 870-873.

Pine, W.E., Pollock, K.H., Hightower, J.E., Kwak, T. J., and Rice, J. A., 2003, A review of tagging methods for estimating fish populations size and components of mortality: Fisheries, v. 28, no. 10, p. 10-23.

Prentice, E.F., McCutcheon, C.S., and Flagg, T.A., 1990, Feasibility of using implantable passive integrated transponder (PIT) tags in salmonids: American Fisheries Society Symposium, v. 7, p. 317-322.

Roussel, J.M., Haro, A., and Cunjak, R.A., 2000, Field test of a new method for tracking small fishes in shallow rivers using passive integrated transponder tags (PIT) technology: Canadian Journal of Fisheries and Aquatic Sciences, v. 57, p. 1326-1329.

Simon, D.C., and Markle, D.F., 2006, Ecology of Upper Klamath Lake shortnose and Lost River suckers – Annual survey of abundance and distribution of age-0 shortnose and Lost River suckers in Upper Klamath Lake, 2005 annual report: Corvallis, Oreg., Oregon Cooperative Research Unit, Department of Fisheries and Wildlife, Oregon State University.

Simon, D.C., and Markle, D.F., 2008, Ecology of Upper Klamath Lake Shortnose and Lost River suckers, Annual survey of abundance and distribution of age 0 shortnose and Lost River suckers in Upper Klamath Lake, 2007 annual report: submitted to the U.S. Geological Survey, Biological Resources Division.

VanderKooi, S.P., and Buelow, K.A., 2003, Nearshore habitat use by endangered juvenile suckers in Upper Klamath Lake, Oregon: Annual Report 2001: U.S. Geological Survey, Western Fisheries Research Center, Klamath Falls Field Station.

VanderKooi, S.P., Hendrixson, H.A., Herring, B.L., and Coshow, R.H., 2007, Nearshore habitat use by endangered juvenile suckers in Upper Klamath Lake, Oregon: Annual Report 2002 – 2003: U.S. Geological Survey, Western Fisheries Research Center, Klamath Falls Field Station.

Ward, D.L., and David, J., 2006, Evaluation of Pit Tag Loss and Tag-induced Mortality in Bluehead Sucker (Catostomus Discobolus): Journal of the Arizona-Nevada Academy of Science, v. 38, p. 74-76.

Ward, D.L., Childs, M.R., and Persons, W.R., 2008, PIT tag retention and tag induced mortality in juvenile bony tail and gila chub: Fisheries Management and Ecology, v. 15, p. 159-161.

Williams, B. K., Nichols, J.D., and Conroy, M.J., 2002, Analysis and management of animal populations: modeling, estimation, and decision making: San Diego, Calif., Academic Press, 817 p.

Zydlewski, G.B., Horton, G., Dubreuil, T., Letcher, B., Casey, S., and Zydlewski, J., 2006, Remote Monitoring of Fish in Small Streams: A Unified Approach Using PIT Tags: Fisheries, v. 31, no. 10, p. 492-502.

Acknowledgments

We thank Kevin Donner, Mark Johnson, Patrick Mirrick, Darin Taylor, Jack Tuomikaski, Corralee Whitsett, Alex Wilkens, and Anna Willard for help with data collection, Alex Wilkens for help with training and field preparations, Dave Simon for help with sucker species identification, Greta Blackwood and Alta Scott for database setup and management and Rip Shively for help with the study design and overall guidance for running the study.